How to Parent a Child with ADHD

*Practical Parenting Strategies
to Help and Promote Positive
Behavior for a Child With ADHD*

Rebecca Solis

Table of Contents

Introduction

P arents look for ADHD remedies in all the wrong ways. ADHD, or attention deficit hyperactivity disorder, is often misdiagnosed and confused because it affects many children (roughly 3-5 percent of all children). In part, parents expect children to misbehave at some stage.

The top five most prevalent problems with parents of children with ADHD are mentioned below. Hopefully, these ADHD responses would also be of assistance in the quest for successful ADHD management and therapies.

ADHD has been identified as a proper condition by reputable pediatric, behavioral, and psychological organizations. Specialists generally acknowledge ADHD as the most common psychiatric illness in children and teenagers, the same as bed-wetting or a lack of ambition. Although it is argued that ADHD has no natural origin and is more difficult to detect than most other physical and psychological disorders in infants, it has solutions to many of the issues that perplexed parents face with the symptoms. It's best to contact a healthcare provider in the field of ADHD for a complete diagnostic interview and tests to ensure you're coping with Attention Deficit Hyperactivity Disorder.

Parents seeking ADHD therapies must first determine if their children exhibit the most common signs of the disorder. Hyperactivity, the extreme failure to concentrate or remain concentrated, and being impulsive and destructive are both central and vital signs. Often, the effects include problems at school, declining academic achievement, battles with other children or adults in control, increased accident rates, and other activities often thought to be triggered by antisocial behavior.

Aside from a comprehensive assessment focused on your child's background (including wellness, family, and school issues), you will be asked to complete ADHD question sheets to identify and diagnose your child, as well as to decide whether he or she is suffering from a different condition.

It is entirely up to you, the adult, to decide. However, federal regulations have made it obligatory for most schools to have adequate facilities to determine whether or not their students have disabilities such as ADHD that can interfere with their schooling. It ensures that children with developmental disabilities aged 3 to 21 receive the appropriate care and public education. ADHD is one of the qualifying criteria for special education, which is lucky. Set up an appointment with your child's homeroom tutor, counselor, or guidance counselor to get the ADHD answers you're looking for. They will either have an individualized education package or add behavior modification in milder symptoms of ADHD.

Will my child develop self-control in a school setting? Behavior therapy seeks to address this issue. Understanding what causes your child's ADHD will help school employees and, in the end, the children with ADHD. They should arrange for specialized seating in the classroom, change some school rules, and enforce a more organized environment to prevent triggers, incorporate programs that can increase social contact with other children, and give regular or weekly updates to parents about their children.

Clinical trials indicate a similarity between ADHD and some mood and anxiety disorders: mood disorders have a 15-20% risk of co-occurring with ADHD while anxiety disorders have a 20-25% chance of overlapping with ADHD. In addition, an infant with ADHD is often more likely to have sleep problems, impairment of motor function, memory and cognitive processing, and be oppositional defiant.

Fortunately, there are now healthy, natural, and prosperous ADHD therapies available. Previously, patients were regularly given drug prescriptions as soon as the child was diagnosed with ADHD. And, indeed, they can be very costly. A healthier choice is to use a more systematic solution that looks at the child as a whole, not just their ADHD symptoms. Take into account their lifestyle, routine, preferences, and physical habits to develop options that are specifically tailored to them. Getting them interested in team activities and crafts, for example, will help them work off extra energy while also encouraging them to engage with other kids their age.

Keep in mind that the bulk of ADHD drugs are stimulants, which may intensify hyperactivity. Choose natural ingredients instead of drugs to satisfy an often posed ADHD question about medication. Look for herbal and botanical extracts in a prepared form that have been shown to minimize restlessness, hyperactivity, nervous mannerisms like fidgeting, and outbursts, such as Hyoscyamus. Consider Tuberculinum, a natural stimulant that deals with irritability; Arsen iod, a herbal extract that encourages balance and helps to relieve agitation and temper tantrums; and Verta alb, to calm hyperactive children's nerves.

Chapter 1:
What is ADHD?

ADHD is a medically recognized disorder with a well-documented neurobiological and neurochemical basis. ADHD primarily involves the frontal, temporal, and prefrontal lobes located in the front of the brain just behind the forehead, part of the cerebrum, and the corpus callosum in the sub-cortical/striatum areas, which the frontal and prefrontal lobes connect. These regions of the brain house the executive and inhibitory function whose dysfunction is at the heart of an ADHD diagnosis.

The basal ganglia control voluntary movement and play an essential role in learning skills. They also maintain our response to reinforcement or rewards, necessary to cause-and-effect learning and if-this-then-that reasoning. It is precisely in charge of controlling motor skills partly by inhibiting particular behaviors and allowing others. The limbic system controls our immediate or automatic responses to our environment. MRI studies, EEG studies, and PET scans have conclusively demonstrated that the ADHD brain is less active and functions differently in these critical areas. These studies have also shown that the brain size in children with ADHD is 3-4% smaller than brain size in children without ADHD.

To further understand the biology of ADHD, it is also important to note the chemical component. The frontal and prefrontal lobe functions are assisted by neurotransmitters (chemical messengers). Two neurotransmitters, in particular, dopamine and norepinephrine, are primarily responsible for the neurochemical component of

ADHD. When both of these chemicals are not adequately regulated, it causes problems. Dopamine is responsible for learning associatively (cause-and-effect) and problem-solving, attention to detail, norepinephrine, the fight-or-flight response, and inhibitory abilities to regulate behavioral and emotional responses directly impacts sustained attention. Both neurotransmitters have a direct relationship with alertness, focus, thought sustainability, effort, and motivation. Reduced activity in the frontal and prefrontal lobes, combined with the improper regulation of dopamine and norepinephrine, results in an essential part of brain functioning being sluggish and the skewing of "stop-and-go" capabilities.

What Exactly Does That Mean?

The observable, identifying symptoms of ADHD are hyperactivity, impulsiveness, and distractibility, beyond what usually is characteristic of children and to the degree that it interferes with the ability to perform daily activities or is disruptive. Children diagnosed with ADHD typically struggle with disorganization, difficulty transitioning from one task to another, a lack of foresight as well as hindsight, difficulty with social skills and reading social cues, frequently feeling overwhelmed and even angry, and lying, cursing, stealing, and blaming others, mainly as the child grows older. They are often described as being driven by a motor or not being able to sit still. Can you now recognize how these earmark characteristics are related to the parts of the brain and chemicals described above?

At the bare minimum, ADHD is known as Attention Deficit Hyperactivity Disorder. That's what the acronym stands. Patients diagnosed with ADHD have trouble focusing their attention and exhibit hyperactive behaviors, along with many other factors that make each patient and their symptoms unique.

As a person with Attention Deficit Hyperactivity Disorder, you might find that you have one aspect of the condition or a little of every element combined. Thus, you could say that ADHD is an umbrella term branching to three more distinct subgroups.

Firstly, you might fall into the predominantly inattentive type of ADHD, which pertains to, as the name suggests, symptoms primarily related to attention span and focus. Secondly, there is the predominantly hyperactive-impulsive type with symptoms affecting impulse control and fidgeting.

Last but not least is the combined type, which is the largest population of the ADHD community. People suffering the combined type aren't exclusively hyperactive or inattentive but have traits that fall in both categories.

All three types can be generalized as ADHD. Still, given that personality disorders are in reality unique to each person, psychiatrists have found that all of us suffering from ADHD have the same issues regarding brain chemistry or efficiency. Still, this same defect presents itself differently in each one of us.

These three categories, inattentive, hyperactive, and combined, are why the exact type of symptoms your ADHD falls under isn't a subtype of ADHD but more like a unique manifestation of your condition caused by the same issues that all other ADHD patients suffer from.

I imagine that they might soon discover more ways that ADHD presents itself to my way of thinking. According to psychiatrists, ADHD symptoms overlap with many symptoms falling under numerous, already existing conditions such as autism, anxiety, borderline personality disorder, and even post-traumatic stress disorder.

To give context on whether you might have ADHD or not, here are just some of the things that ADHD patients said they have to endure:

- Restlessness
- Inattention
- Hyperactivity
- Impulsivity
- Chronic procrastination
- Distractibility
- Difficulty organizing in all aspects

Always late

Is ADHD A Personality Disorder?

However, it does begin in childhood, suggesting that it can't develop suddenly or predictably even in adulthood.

Benefits of ADHD

A message to the afflicted: feel no despair or shame in being who you are, for there is a reason behind your suffering and great opportunities underlie your condition. You are the catalyst that will change the world for the better. We have gone through what we did to show the world that we can still lead loving and happy lives with all our difficulties.

ADHD as a Strength

For so long, I thought of my ADHD as a weakness. I saw it as something that held me back from others and made me feel as though I wasn't as good as my peers. I thought I was dumb, anxious and overall, not as fun of a person as anyone else.

I might not have had as easy of a time focusing in class, but that didn't mean the papers I turned in weren't as eloquent or filled with valuable information. I would struggle to carry specific conversations, but that didn't mean I still couldn't make my friends laugh.

We must look for ways that ADHD has enhanced our lives and the lives of those around us, even if in small ways. Life might have been easier had I grown up without ADHD, but it would have led me down a different path, and who knows what that might have looked like. Accepting our ADHD is crucial in realizing that it is what got us to this place, and in the end, that's a good thing.

Successful People Who Used Their ADHD to Accomplish

Numerous successful individuals have used their ADHD as an advantage and can accomplish amazing things in life. Anytime you feel "less than" or as if you're not good enough, remember that all of these successful people overcame stigma, and their struggles, to find the happy life they deserve:

- Simone Biles, Olympic gymnast
- Justin Timberlake, Emmy Award-winning singer
- Michael Phelps, Olympic swimmer
- Jim Carrey, Grammy-winning actor, and comedian
- Pete Rose, Major League baseball player
- Channing Tatum, award-winning actor
- Ryan Gosling, Golden Globe-winning actor

If they can lead incredible lives despite (or maybe because of) their ADHD diagnosis, what's stopping you from doing the same?

Chapter 2:
Causes of ADHD

S ince attention-deficit impulsivity disorder (ADHD) signs lack of attention, aggression, and hyperactivity impact a kid's potential to understand and even get together with many others, certain may believe that the behavior of an ADHD child is triggered by either a lack of knowledge, a dysfunctional home environment, or perhaps too much tv. Evidence currently shows ADHD is primarily a neurological disease. Some external conditions, though, may also play a part. Here we distinguish fact from opinion about ADHD reasons.

Pesticides

Investigation suggests a possible link between pesticides and ADHD. A 2010 research in pediatricians found higher rates of ADHD in kids with higher concentrations of outside organophosphate in the urine; an insecticide utilized on goods. Another study in 2010 had shown that people with a higher concentration of organophosphate in urine were much more likely to have a kid with ADHD

Drinking and Smoking in Pregnancy Period

Deadly alcohol and tobacco exposure are believed to play a role in ADHD.

Exposure to Lead

Neurotoxic substance lead has been eliminated from several households and classrooms, but there are still signs of it everywhere. A 2009 research showed that kids with ADHD appeared to have higher blood leads than other adolescents. "Lead may be toxic to the development of brain tissue could have maintained impact on the development of exposing kids to such substances at an early age," said Leavitt, practicing under Richard Oelberger's supervision. "Still, such exposure is unlikely to account for brain differences advancement in the large majority of ADHD kids and teens."

Food Flavorings

After research, several European states have banned specific additives, which connected impulsivity in small kids to food only with blends of some and sodium preservative benzoic. When utilized "correctly," the FDA said that dietary supplements are safe, but most additives are not required to be labeled on the packaging. Experts believe that a small percentage of kids will benefit from avoiding brightly colored foods that are processed and appear to have even more preservatives. "Seek advice with your kid's doctor before you put your kid on a specific diet," Leavitt says. Reducing the utilize of such preservatives may not contribute to excitable behavior; in ADHD, many factors play a crucial role.

Sugar Intake

Mother and father often blame the excitable behavior for sugar, but it is time to stop it. "The numerous overpowering studies have failed to show behavioral changes in kids due to sugar intake," said Dr. Wolraich. An investigation published in the journal of such unusual kid development found that women who thought that sugar was given to their kids assessed the behavior of their kids as being more excitable than moms who were told that a sugar substitute was given to their kids — irrespective as to whether their kids ingested natural sugar. So if you are worried regarding caloric intake or limit sugar, dental cavities, ADHD isn't the cause.

Video Games or TV

There's no evidence that ADHD is caused by too much TV as well as video game time, even if the research has suggested that school-age and college and high school-age learners who spent a lot of time next to a screen have much more attention difficulties than others who do not. The continuous exposure to television and video games will, in principle, make it easier for kids to lose focus. And yet experts stress that screen time alone is not the only cause of ADHD. There's an affiliation between it and the number of hours young kids watch TV as well as play computer games. Still, much more study is needed to determine whether it's a causal connection or because kids with ADHD simply gravitate more towards those actions," said Dr. Wolraich.

Bad Kid Parenting

Symptoms of ADHD may be associated with disruptive or inappropriate conduct, and it's not unusual to pin a kid's actions on the mother. But there is no significant evidence, as per the statewide counseling center at ADHD, that authoritative parenting leads to ADHD.

"Although authoritative parenting and social conditions can exacerbate ADHD habits, authoritative parenting is not the trigger of ADHD," said Leavitt. Family and friends may have specific behavioral boundaries, using incentive and behavioral outcome strategies. They have a simple range of goals to help minimize symptoms of ADHD. But on the other side, the side effects can be made worse by a complex living environment and parents who fail to admit ADHD as a medical condition.

Injuries of Brain

"Head trauma that occurs from a heavy stroke to the head, either neurological disorder, an injury, or illness may trigger inattention issues and impaired control of physical function and tendencies," Leavitt notes. But due to the community mental wellbeing Institute, kids with some forms of brain damage can have signs close to ADHD. But since only a limited percentage of adolescents with ADHD also experienced brain trauma, this is not deemed a significant risk indicator.

Heredity

The research clearly shows that caregivers pass on the ADHD, not the parental method. "ADHD possesses a very proud legacy," Smith affirms. "It is perhaps one of the greatest inherited psychological conditions." Indeed, a kid is 4 times more likely to have had a close relative who was also diagnosed with ADHD, and the results of various twin studies signify that ADHD frequently occurs in families. Continuing work seeks to classify the genes that are responsible more for ADHD.

Overdiagnosis for ADHD

Since there is no final check for ADHD, caregivers, physicians, and educators often argue if ADHD is now over-diagnosed. A few say that physicians are too fast to diagnose behavioral issues in a kid as ADHD without considering many other possible reasons. For example, researchers at the Colorado state institute have found that kids may be accidentally medicated with ADHD when they are, in fact, only less bright. According to Dr. Wolraich, "Many other pieces of evidence are underrecognized with ADHD."

Exposure to Chemicals

Although cigarettes, alcohol, and insecticides can be an issue, observers will also look at other toxins. For example, researchers at the Boston school of public safety identified a correlation between the polyfluoroalkyl compound's industrial substances typically utilized in items such as stain-resistant coatings and packaged food and ADHD. In addition, Phthalates found in things such as gadgets, packaged food, and cosmetics were also associated with ADHD. Again, as with other causes, the proof points to a connection but it cannot conclude that such chemicals lead to ADHD.

Chapter 3:
Common Myths about ADHD

M isconceptions and myths can be found in every minute portion of life, and thus ADHD is no different. However, when myths and misconceptions start forming deeper roots in society, it can make the whole situation a significant problem. People start believing them, and the ultimate result is that you won't differentiate between true and false. Misconceptions and myths regarding any kind of disease can result in serious harm. So, it is essential to debunk such myths and just see the problem in the natural light. Also, myths and misconceptions can sometimes make the treatment procedure quite tiresome.

Real Disorder

ADHD has consistently been recognized as a severe disorder by most medical professionals, psychological and psychiatric experts, and organizations and associations in the United States. Some influential organizations are APA or American Psychiatric Association, NIH or National Institute of Health, and the Center for Disease Control and Prevention. Like other severe medical conditions, a medical expert or a doctor cannot just confirm the diagnosis of ADHD with the help of imaging and laboratory test. Indeed, there is no proper test for diagnosing ADHD; certain specific and transparent criteria require to be met for the diagnosis. Mental health professionals and doctors can use these criteria and detailed history and information regarding the concerned person's behaviors to provide a reliable diagnosis.

Another critical factor is that the symptoms of ADHD are not always defined clearly. ADHD exists on a proper sequence of behaviors. All of us experience some sort of problems regarding focusing and attention at times. However, for a person suffering from ADHD, all these symptoms might turn out to be severe enough that they can easily hamper their daily functioning. ADHD symptoms might also resemble some other conditions. Therefore, undiagnosed or pre-existing medical problems need to be recognized before a diagnosis of ADHD.

ADHD is Often Over-Diagnosed

The evidence regarding this is kind of mixed. According to annual data, there is an increase in the diagnosis of ADHD in children in the U.S. But the reports also state that the rates of other severe conditions, like anxiety, depression, and autism have also shown an increase. Talking about ADHD specifically, various studies have demonstrated that the situation might get under-diagnosed in some instances where the overall symptoms are much less noticeable. A prominent example gathered from the evidence shows that ADHD might manifest differently in female children.

While female children with ADHD have fewer chances of showing any hyperactive symptoms, they might still have some impairment of significant focus and mental tasks. A wide range of studies has suggested that female children are less likely to get diagnosed and receive any treatment related to ADHD than male children.

Other studies suggest that ADHD is most of the time over-diagnosed, however, particularly in boys. Increased rates of ADHD in male children might be partly because of the stereotypes regarding male behavior; for instance, boys tend to act out physically. Boys might also be more likely to show disruptive and ADHD symptoms, which directly enhances the chances that teachers, parents, and doctors will notice all their behaviors. It has been found that ethnic, socioeconomic, and racial factors also play some role in the disparity in the treatment and diagnosis of ADHD. According to a study from the year 2016, white children are most likely to be diagnosed with ADHD and receive treatment for the same. Although the researchers find these findings to imply over-diagnosis, they suggest that under-treatment and under-diagnosis of Latino and African American children with ADHD could be a more specific interpretation of the gathered data.

Another research proposed that ADHD in adults is also over-diagnosed. It is often suggested that adults might get diagnosed with the symptoms of ADHD because of the medicalization of their typical personality variations and life experiences. In some cases, other types of learning disabilities or mental health conditions are often misdiagnosed as the symptoms of ADHD. The primary risk involved with the over-diagnosis of ADHD is unnecessary treatment along with stimulant medication. Although the related drugs can work as an effective treatment for ADHD, they might be misused when provided to someone who does not require them.

ADHD Can Only Be Found in Children

The ADHD symptoms require to be present by the age of seven to meet the diagnosis criteria adequately. However, some people often remain undiagnosed until they reach adulthood. It is not uncommon for some parents to get diagnosed with ADHD along with their children at the same point in time. As any adult starts learning in detail about the actual condition, they might begin to recognize the traits of ADHD and the related behaviors in themselves. While thinking about their childhood, they might just realize that the struggles they faced at school were most probably the result of problems related to attention that went untreated or unnoticed. For children and parents, proper diagnosis at any point might seem like a relief. Getting the ability to put the symptoms under some kind of names while also knowing that there are ways to manage them might be reassuring properly.

Many children diagnosed with the symptoms of ADHD might continue to showcase the symptoms even as teens and adults. However, the general nature of the symptoms might change as they grow. For instance, the hyperactive nature of behaviors that are common in kids tends to reduce with age. However, distractibility, inattention, and restlessness might persist into their adulthood. ADHD in adults, which is managed poorly, might often result in chronic problems in relationships and work. Untreated and undiagnosed ADHD can also be linked with substance misuse, depression, and anxiety.

ADHD is the Result of Bad Parenting

Parents of ADHD children might often worry that they will be blamed for their children's behaviors. However, the overall condition is not caused by bad parenting strictly. Whether they are suffering from the symptoms of ADHD or not, any child can get affected adversely by critical and punitive parenting or a chaotic home. All such factors might make the whole situation more challenging for the children to cope with the problems of ADHD; however, they are not the primary cause of the condition. With that said, parents might want to consider adapting their parenting style to support their ADHD child in a better way.

Symptoms of ADHD is Hyperactivity

The "attention deficit" portion of the name has resulted in misunderstandings regarding the general nature of the condition and has also perpetuated various myths regarding the symptoms. Hyperactive behaviors can only be found in the predominantly hyperactive-impulsive type and cannot be found mainly in the predominantly inattentive one. ADHD of the predominantly inattentive nature is often referred to as attention-deficit disorder or ADD to reduce any kind of confusion. Any individual who showcases inattentive symptoms might appear easily distracted and daydreamy. They might also be careless, forgetful, and disorganized. ADHD of this type is overlooked most of the time. It is mainly because it is less disruptive than the hyperactive one. But the related symptoms can still be dreadful to the one who is experiencing all of them.

While any child who has ADHD will not outgrow the disorder typically, sometimes adults report growing out of the behaviors of hyperactive nature that they had in their childhood. In some cases, hyperactivity might get replaced by apathy and restlessness.

People who have ADHD Cannot Focus at All

Provided the condition's name, it might be confusing for some people to see someone with ADHD/ADD intently focusing on any activity. It will be more accurate to describe the portion of attention-deficit as difficulty in regulating concentration in place of the ability to pay any attention. Although individuals who have ADHD face problems organizing, completing, and focusing on tasks, it is not uncommon for them to get absorbed in all those activities they find interesting.

Hyperfocusing at such a sustained level can indicate when someone has ADHD.

Addiction and Drug Abuse

There is a significant concern that the stimulant medications used for treating problems of ADHD can result in substance misuse. But it has been found from research that ADHD, when left untreated, can easily enhance a person's risk for substance use disorder. Depression or anxiety can also result from untreated ADHD. An individual might misuse illicit and licit drugs to medicate their symptoms of ADHD along with any other secondary nature of the psychological condition. It has also been found that all those who receive proper treatment for ADHD come with a lower percentage of substance misuse, along with stimulant medication.

Medication Can Completely Treat ADHD

Medication cannot cure the symptoms of ADHD. However, it can readily help manage the symptoms when administered under the guidance of mental health professionals. ADHD can be regarded as a lifelong and chronic condition. If someone gets prescribed to have ADHD medication during their childhood, they might have to continue consuming the same as an adult. People might just carry on with the same symptoms as adults that they had as children. The symptoms might also lessen or just change with time. Developmental alterations in the brain can explain all such changes partly. However, they might also be the reflection of the ways someone has gained knowledge about coping.

Individuals with ADHD might often develop organizational skills and coping strategies to help them move on with the condition. They can expand and continue to build up all these skills throughout their lives. They might also decide to pair the same along with medications.

ADHD Develops When Children are Lazy

It can be regarded as a proper way of demeaning the actual problem as ADHD is not a result of a lack of motivation or laziness. It is an actual medical problem that needs to be adequately addressed. When your child is suffering from the symptoms of ADHD, it is not the case that he/she is not trying to focus on things. In actuality, they are giving their best to do so. However, they cannot end up doing so. If you are just asking your child to concentrate more and being rude/angry on the, as they are not trying, it is worthless.

It is similar to getting mad at someone who cannot see something while being blind in reality. Your child's attitude is not the main factor trying to affect the child's attentive power. It is only because of some physical differences in their brains that they cannot do or see things like any other child. Expecting them to perform or behave like the rest of the children when they are not even built-in that way is foolish.

Chapter 4:
How Do I Recognize ADHD?

T question always is: How do I spot a child with ADHD? My child is active and is so full of energy. Does that make them ADHD? All these questions are among the chief concerns of parents everywhere, and it is a valid concern since most children are active and full of energy. However, when it comes to ADHD in children, it usually concerns their responses or lack of spontaneous reactions, which involve everything from movement to speech and inattentiveness. We all know children who can never seem to listen or sit still, children who can't seem to understand and follow directions despite how clearly it has been outlined to them. ADHD kids also blurt out unnecessary comments at odd times.

Not all of them have ADHD, and not all of them are troublemakers. Whatever the case, thorough observation and assessment are required.

Signs and Symptoms

The various signs and symptoms of ADHD can be present for any child. To diagnose ADHD, the child's pediatrician will need to evaluate your child using a set of criteria. ADHD is commonly diagnosed among children even before they become teenagers, and on average, when they are 7 years old. Older children may exhibit some symptoms of ADHD, but these symptoms are showcased in more elaborate signs when they were younger.

Common signs to look out for:

1. They have a self-focused behavior

Among the most common signs of ADHD is that they cannot recognize people's needs and desires. This often leads to our following two common symptoms: interrupting and trouble to wait their turn.

2. Constant interruption

For children with ADHD, a self-focused behavior often interrupts other people while talking or just rudely joining conversations or games they're not part of.

3. Can't seem to wait for their turn

Children with ADHD often have difficulty waiting for their turn during school or games or basically anything that requires waiting.

4. Emotional turmoil

They also have trouble keeping their emotions in check. Very often, children with ADHD have outbursts at odd times, and they can also whip up temper tantrums unknowingly.

5. Fidgetiness

While most children's attention span is short and they also can't still for too long, children with ADHD usually start fidgeting easily, begin squirming in their seats, and just can't sit still even for a few seconds.

6. Problems playing quietly

Because they often fidget, it also makes it difficult for children with ADHD to engage in quiet and leisurely activities.

7. Unfinished tasks

Another commonality among children with ADHD is the interest in many different things but the inability to finish them. They could often be asked to do chores or start projects or even complete their homework, but they never complete a task. Instead, they move on to the next thing that interests them. While most kids do this, parents should focus on how frequently or how fast a child switches their attention to something else.

8. Lack of focus

This brings us to the following symptom, which is the apparent lack of focus and attention. Children with ADHD usually have even shorter attention spans even when a person is speaking to them. They will tell you that they heard you, but when you ask them to repeat what has been revealed, they cannot tell you what it is.

9. Avoiding tasks that require extensive mental effort

The lack of focus can also contribute to a child avoiding activities that need prolonged focus and attention, such as doing homework.

10. Mistakes

The lack of focus also means that they have trouble or difficulty in following instructions, not because they are stupid or lazy. Usually, the lack of focus just leads to careless mistakes, but this does not mean that the child is lazy or not intelligent.

11. Daydreaming

While all kids can be loud and noisy, you would find that kids with ADHD are not always audible, boisterous, or rowdy. Another sign of ADHD is that they are often quieter and less involved in classroom activities or at home. A child with ADHD may often daydream, stare into space, and are often oblivious to what is happening around them.

12. Trouble getting organized

They also have trouble keeping track of their activities and their tasks. This usually results in problems at school or among their peers because prioritizing is often tricky for children with ADHD.

13. Forgetfulness

In daily activities, children with ADHD may be forgetful in doing their homework and their chores. They also often lose things such as their toys and such.

14. Symptoms in multiple settings

There will be more than one setting where a child with ADHD displays symptoms. For example, in school and at home, they can lose concentration. It is just not in school that they seem disinterested.

Looking forward

At some point, all children demonstrate some of these behaviors, and all of them are normal. From daydreaming to constant interruptions, these are all the kinds of things children do. However, you need to investigate getting an evaluation for your child if they often display signs of ADHD and their behavior begins to affect how they respond to their environment and their success in school. Their behavior leads to negative interactions with their friends and peers.

That said, ADHD is not a cause for worry. It is treatable, and for children diagnosed with ADHD, you need to review all the treatment options available. Set up a time with your child's pediatrician or doctor who will recommend a psychologist for an evaluation and the next course of action. Essentially, ADHD symptoms can be categorized into three groups: inattention, impulsivity, and hyperactivity.

For a child to have ADHD, this means these symptoms are frequent and constant. It is always there and not because of any elements around the child. Usually, it could be a teacher who first notices the inattention, impulsivity, or hyperactivity; these observations would then be brought forward to the parent for further attention. At other times, the pediatrician could bring up this issue with the parent after routine visits. Usually, the pediatrician would ask questions such as:

"Are you concerned with specific behaviors your child is showing in school or at home?

"Are you concerned with the way they play with their friends?"

"Is your child happy in school?"

"How is your child doing in school?"

Causes of ADHD

Research on ADHD has shown that several factors could cause it; brain anatomy and function lower activity levels in the brain, which controls attention and activity, could be associated with ADHD. In some cases, ADHD can be caused by severe head injuries.

It could be genes and heredity. A child with ADHD is 1 out of 4 likely to have an ADHD parent. Another close family member, including a sibling, is also expected to have ADHD. There are times when ADHD is diagnosed concurrently in a child in a parent. The risk of developing ADHD rises with prematureness.

The risk of developing ADHD rises with prenatal factors such as alcohol or consuming nicotine. The chances of developing ADHD rise with prenatal factors such as alcohol or consuming nicotine. Toxins in the atmosphere can, in sporadic cases, cause ADHD. For example, lead may affect the development and actions of children.

There is no evidence to support claims that ADHD is caused by:

- Excessive sugar in food and drinks
- Additives in food
- Having allergies
- Vaccines and immunizations

Why do so many children have ADHD?

There have been a growing number of children seeking ADHD medication. There is no substantial evidence whether more kids with ADHD or more kids are diagnosed with ADHD than before. However, more and more children with ADHD are treated for a more extended period.

Based on national data findings, ADHD affects at least 9.4 percent of children in the U.S. ages 2 to 17. This includes children ages 2 to 5, which comprise 2.4%, and school-age children taking 4 to 12%. In addition, girls and boys with this disorder usually show additional mental disorder symptoms and have language and learning problems. Nevertheless, better treatment, therapy, and more robust and comprehensive diagnosing methods enable more and more children and even adults to have access to more accurate diagnoses and receiving the proper guidance, treatment, and help.

Chapter 5:
Accepting Your Child's ADHD

I t's one thing to be informed about ADHD and learn all you can to help your child better. But actually, coping with an ADHD child daily can be very stressful and frustrating. It may be more so for you if you are the primary caregiver, but never forget that the stress can take its toll on your family as well. That's why the first thing you need to do is establish strategies to help you and your family cope and accept the situation.

Moving Forward

Learning that your child has ADHD triggers a rollercoaster of emotions; fear, grief, worry, anger and guilt, and shock. Then, how is my family going to manage? Take time to get over your initial shock and grief, but after that, it's time to get down to business. The first thing that you and your family must do is accept that the situation will not go away overnight or anytime soon, for that matter. Your day-to-day life needs to more or less be structured around your child, and everyone must do their part.

How to Cope Emotionally as a Parent

Let's be honest. Discovering that your child has ADHD is highly traumatic. You may have suspected it. You may have guessed that the symptoms and behavior your child has been displaying were signs that he has ADHD. Nevertheless, the official diagnosis from the doctor is always a shock.

However, sincere acceptance of your child's condition is an essential part of your emotional healing as a parent.

The following are the best ways you can overcome the emotional struggle and find peace in acceptance.

1. Allow yourself to mourn. As parents, we all have bright visions of what our children will be: well-behaved, high achievers at school, popular with friends, and praised by teachers. This vision is harshly shattered when a child is diagnosed with ADHD. Realizing that he will never behave like other children break your heart. Give yourself time to grieve, and don't bury your emotions. It's okay to cry and feel sad. Acknowledging these feelings is the only way to release them.

2. Stop rejecting who your child is. Your first thoughts will probably be angry ones: Why can't my child be like everyone else? Why does it have to be him? What have I done to deserve this? What has my child done to deserve this? Acknowledge those thoughts, but don't believe them. Instead, challenge the thoughts.

3. Do you blame him for having ADHD? On the contrary, you probably love him even more and want to do everything in your power to protect and shelter him. You love your child no matter who he is. This is another step towards acceptance.

4. See your child's positive strengths and be grateful that he is healthy and robust. ADHD does not disqualify a child from being gifted and talented in many areas. On the contrary, kids with ADHD are incredibly gifted and creative due to their natural vitality and energy. Focus on

these strengths and let them become your source of pride and joy.

5. Don't feel guilty. Guilt is usually the parent's first reaction when they learn that their child has a disease or disorder. You are not responsible. It's not your fault. It's normal to feel guilty. Get over it!

6. Stop when you catch yourself fighting reality. Rejecting reality is a lost battle. This is when you find yourself hoping against hope that your child will suddenly start behaving differently or that his symptoms will suddenly go away. You may even reject the fact that he has ADHD at all, thinking it was a misdiagnosis, and rush to get a second and a third opinion.

Ignoring the facts is emotionally damaging because a child with ADHD will not outgrow it overnight and never behave in the way you expect him to. When you catch yourself having these thoughts, stop immediately, and ground yourself in reality.

All of this aims to change your perspective on the process and accept your child's condition emotionally. Now that you are on the way to acceptance, it's time to incorporate more practical coping strategies.

1. Manage your stress. Stress is the number one struggle you will face when raising a child with ADHD. Unfortunately, it is one you will meet daily. Unless you have techniques to help you lower your stress, the effects on your physical and mental health can be severe. Managing stress will also help you be more tolerant and calmer when dealing with your child and less prone to anger or frustration. The more drama you can avoid, the better for you and your child.

2.   Join a support group. Encouragement and support from parents in the same situation are crucial. Search for these groups online or on social media platforms—you will be surprised to discover how many there are. This is a beautiful way to share your problems and concerns, exchange advice, tips, and experiences with other parents. If the group is local, you can even arrange to meet regularly and introduce your children to each other. Many support groups also agree to lectures by experts to stay on top of the latest information on ADHD. They also organize activities and outings for families. Knowing you are not alone and that your problems are common to many other people will help keep your resolve strong.

Helping Your Child Cope

Do not wait for him to learn that he has ADHD from a teacher or classmate or by overhearing a conversation. First of all, he will think it more severe than it is and that you are hiding something terrible from him. Second, your child may lose trust in you. It is your responsibility to be the first to inform your child about his condition and to explain the facts. A simple explanation in simple words is sufficient for very young children.

- Tell your child that he has a problem called ADHD
- Explain the symptoms in simple terms, telling him that he will have difficulty sitting still, waiting for his turn, or focusing for a long time and that he has to work harder than other kids to do that.
- Explain that all children are different and have different needs. For example, some children like to sit still and do

quiet activities while others, like himself, have more energy and move around more. Also, tell him that while some children have to sit at the front of the class to hear and see well, he may need to listen more carefully to understand what the teacher is explaining.

- Explain what ADHD IS NOT. For example, it's not lazy or stupid or badly behaved and hat, it's not something to be ashamed of. This is very important because, sadly, these things may be said to your child by other people.

- If your child is taking medication, explain that it will help him focus better. In addition, you can discuss other children you may know who are taking medication, such as asthma so that your child is reassured that medication is not a bad thing.

- Get the point across that all people have things they are better at than others. Discuss your child's strengths, such as drawing well, running fast, being funny, etc.

- Keep your explanation simple and explain only the basics.

- Give your child honest answers to any questions he may have. Do not raise the child's expectations. Tell him that both of you have to work hard together, and he will start to get better slowly, but that will take some time.

- Discuss the strategies you will follow together to help him deal with ADHD.

Tips to Helping Your Family Cope

If you have other children, the first thing you need to do is explain that their sibling has ADHD. They were simplifying as required depending on their ages. Let them know that you expect them to help their brother or sister whenever they can and to never, ever taunt him about his condition. Never hesitate to enforce strict discipline when this is done. The whole family should follow the following strategies. Lead by example, and your other children will learn to behave and interact with their siblings.

- Celebrate the "pros" of ADHD. Children with ADHD often have unique gifts that can be supported and encouraged. Creativity, spontaneity, energy, and enthusiasm are some examples. Point out these gifts to your child often.
- Help your child whenever appropriate. For example, when he is struggling with a specific task. Encourage your family to help with homework and engage in therapy whenever possible.
- Structure family and household rules and activities that will allow your child to succeed. For example, giving him shorter chores to accomplish, making a list of things he needs to do to cross each one-off—structure, and schedule playtime with siblings to engage in the games he likes.

Monitor playtimes if possible so that the child does not get over-excited. Be on the alert for fights breaking out between siblings or other children and intervene at once. When assigning larger tasks, enlist a sibling to help your child succeed in complete them.

Chapter 6:
Identifying ADHD Symptoms for Proper Treatment

N aughty, obedient, and spectacular—these are only a few words used to describe people who have impulsivity, indifference, and hyperactivity. To the untrained eye, these are only destructive behaviors. But is it valid? Does it have to be more of what you see?

Attention deficit hyperactivity disease is a condition that can be hyperactive, impulsive, and inattentive for both children and adults. This is a developmental disorder, usually before a child turns seven, and when not controlled, it can persist into adulthood. Therefore, understanding various ADHD signs is of the highest importance for proper attention deficit hyperactivity disorder. In addition, it helps you to see if you or one of your loved ones has ADHD.

These are split into three for a better understanding of the specific ADHD symptoms in children. The first is inattentive signs and symptoms that occur when the child makes several careless errors, is distracted, and has difficulty keeping focused. The child also pays no attention to details, and when you talk to them, they seem not to listen. There will also be trouble following directions, and they have problems arranging and preparing their things in advance.

Next, in the case of the signs of hyperactive ADHD, the child is constantly fidgeting, is unable to hold still, walks quickly, talks loudly, has a short temper, and is restless. Finally, premature signs of ADHD are seen when the child does not care, when they cannot wait for their turn during plays when they are on track when they speak, they disrupt others, and they cannot control emotions.

Adults with hyperactivity disorder with attention deficit have symptoms of ADHD different from those of children. One of the most common ADHD symptoms seen in adults is difficulty focusing. They are easily distracted, still, fail to complete their tasks even worldly, their listening capacity is weak, and they often miss specifics. Some people will be hyperfocused or tend to become too absorbed in rewarding things.

Like children, adults also show disorder and forgetfulness. Whether at home or work, a person with ADHD may find it challenging to plan and typically postpone their tasks. Forgetting appointments, misplacing, chronic lateness, and difficulties with job completion are also some of the most common symptoms of ADHD in adults. In addition, there is also impulsiveness in which poor self-control is manifested. Hyperactivity can also be seen in specific individuals, as well as anger control problems.

Such signs of ADHD are often misunderstood and ignored, and many people believe that a child is outgrowing them or that an adult has only some issues. But if you know that these symptoms of ADHD are chronic and continue to get worse, it's high time you got treatment. Proper treatment is then taken to manage these symptoms.

Controlling Your Child's ADHD Symptoms Naturally

Children were overwhelmingly diagnosed with ADHD. And over the last 20 years, the numbers have increased. As a result, children with ADHD symptoms (hyperactivity, lack of focus, and learning problems) usually end up in a doctor's office with anxious parents who don't know where else to go.

Families often leave the physician's office on a drug prescription like Adderall or Strattera and hope that the symptoms will be managed early. Nevertheless, medicines are not the only option. Most natural treatments are gaining popularity.

Diet regulation

The first step for a parent who does not want to take medication from his child is to reduce any symptoms that could affect his diet. The triggers include milk, processed foods, and sugary snacks with tea and additives. While the complete elimination of these foods was once strongly suggested, studies begin to show that dietary intervention works best when combined with other policies.

Doctors of behavioral therapy have a long list of recommended conduct therapy with ADHD drugs, although this is not always a tool. Parents interested in improving their children's organizational and social skills have now become very popular. Comportment therapy techniques include the introduction of reward systems with rewards and consequences.

It is eliminating distractions that make it difficult to focus.

Continuous training of parents on how to correct behavioral problems. Alternative treatments for symptoms of ADHD: Some parents use alternate therapies to reduce symptoms of ADHD. Meditation and progressive relaxation are two therapies that show positive results (a technique that calms the body).

One advantage of meditation is the ability to focus more on both adults and children. Digital guided infant meditations take into account the limitations of a child sitting still. You will gradually reduce the ADHD symptoms over time by teaching your child to slow down and calm down. It means tensing the muscles of your body and then relaxing one part of your body at a time. It should be done at bedtime every night.

ADHD Symptoms – Lack of Attention and Concentration

Before you know what the symptoms of ADHD are, you should know precisely what the complete form of ADHD is. It is called the Hyperactivity Disorder of Attention Deficit. There are many ADHD types if you check on the internet or simply contact a physician. These symptoms of ADHD are found primarily in familiar children and adolescents. But it is also possible for even adults to manifest these symptoms.

For example, one of the symptoms an adult can experience is restlessness without working hard or doing anything else. In adults, problems arise from interpersonal relationships. The forms of ADHD are essentially three different types, including the most common type of mixed ADHD. Inattentive ADHD is also referred to as ADD, which results in a loss of concentration and contractions. For information purposes only, you should know the ADHD symptoms and manage them when diagnosed with ADHD.

The symptoms are often divided into three categories, including hyperactivity, carelessness, and impulsiveness. The child may not show inattention unless they enter into the crowded and challenging school environment. The same symptom applies to adults in social situations or the workplace. The typical symptom of ADHD is that the sufferers find it very difficult to work efficiently. They also have difficulty paying attention to specific subjects or information and making stupid mistakes at work or school. When diagnosed, you can distract yourself easily from the noises others try to avoid. To do a specific task because of less focus.

It is difficult for a child or an adult to complete paperwork or schoolwork in concentration. The noticeable symptoms of ADHD are changes in day-to-day habits, neglecting essential things such as meetings, appointments with a physician, forgetting to call someone, and more.

The child cannot do their homework on time or study during examination times due to lack of care and concentration, failing, and even does not take part in tasks where they need to concentrate. For adults, the inattention symptoms that occur under the symptoms of ADHD must be supported because even adults lack the concentration and attention they need at work or meetings and in social environments. Hyperactivity is the other symptom of ADHD.

This symptom is present mainly in pre-school children before the age of seven. If you see that person diagnosed with them, they are nervous while sitting or are restless, so they often walk or go and have the most extraordinary restlessness after running or climbing. They find it difficult to play games or keep themselves involved in an activity. Most of them are rushed or ready to go to a given place and always speak minimally and provide reasons for particular contact.

Chapter 7:
Principles to Raise an ADHD Child

Any tools, therapies, or methods you decide to use with your child will not be very beneficial unless implemented within a specific framework. This framework will create an optimal environment for your child to thrive and succeed. One important keyword is structure. The structure is vital for children with ADHD, as you will learn.

The 5 Cs of parenting

They are basic guidelines for raising all kids, but they are particularly ideal - and necessary - for children with ADHD. The 5 Cs are the basic framework within which you will implement all the other strategies and methods to help your child.

#1 Consistency

- Consistent schedules and rules make children feel safe. This applies even more to kids with ADHD because they feel uncomfortable with change and disruptions to their daily routines.
- Consistency means both a structured daily schedule as well as consistent rewards and discipline for behavior.
- Be very clear about the rules and schedules you set. Explain to your child what each management entails and that he is expected to obey rules and finish scheduled tasks.
- A daily schedule should include times for homework, chores, meals, T.V., and play. The program should consist of the

whole family and not just the child, making him feel isolated and more likely to rebel. Scheduling one-to-one time for doing activities with your child is different. It will make him feel unique and essential.

- Put schedules on a bulletin board in your child's room or stick them on the fridge where he can see them constantly.

However, letting him off the hook should not become a habit. Instead, schedule another time for him to complete unfinished tasks, for example, or tell him that he will be disciplined the next time he breaks a rule – and keep your word. Telling a child to tidy his room simply be too overwhelming for him. Break the task into a list of steps such as

- picking up toys
- Making his bed
- Organizing a shelf or cupboard
- Hanging up clothes

This will prevent your child from feeling confused and frustrated and prevent you from enforcing unnecessary discipline.

#2 Self-Control

This is possibly the biggest challenge for parents who have an ADHD child. There will be times when you will be tempted just to lose it and scream and rant at your child for being so difficult. But you must muster every ounce of self-control to remain steady and calm.

When you are near breaking point, remember this: expecting your child to be organized, focused, and calm is like throwing someone who can't swim into the middle of the ocean and telling him to swim to shore. Remember that your child is struggling to do his best and that he may be just as frustrated as you are. Compassion and empathy are the keys to keeping your cool

- Always remember that you are your child's first role model. When he sees you behaving with quiet self-control in stressful situations, he will learn from you and control himself better.
- As a parent, you need to be the one who keeps everybody grounded when your child is challenging.
- Despite structure and schedule, things on the home front will not always be rosy. When a difficult situation with your child begins to arise, be prepared to handle it calmly and firmly. Self-control can often create the only barrier to chaos in your family

Another suggestion is to give yourself time-out when things get too overwhelming. Leave the room, go for a walk around the block or take a quick shower. Finally, do not confront your child when you are angry.

#3 Compassion

Just because your child has ADHD does not mean he is deficient in understanding and sensitivity. On the contrary, children with ADHD are susceptible and emotional. Your child or example understands that he can no. He may also be criticized by others or taunted by peers to feel he can't do anything right.

- You need to be your child's anchor of understanding and compassion. It is crucial for the child to feel that you accept him completely the way he is and deeply loved. This will compensate for a lot of the negativity that he may encounter outside of the home,

- Express your love and confidence in your child often, even when you are forced to discipline him. For example, when you tell him that he can't go outside to play because he didn't finish his homework. Explain that you are forced to punish him because you love him and want him to do well in school.

- Knowing that you are on his side will encourage him to overcome his negative feelings and accept himself.

#4 Celebration

- A child with ADHD thrives on praise and reassurance that he is doing well, so always look for opportunities to express your pride in him.

- Praise your child when he completes tasks successfully and when he does things without having to be reminded.

- Celebrate your child's talents with praise and encouragement. For example, frame and hang his artwork on your walls, or share it on Facebook. In addition, place things he has made, such as sculptures and crafts, on a prominent shelf in your home and encourage him to add to them.

- Family members should express their appreciation and celebration of the child's uniqueness.

- Keep praise specific. For example, "You have such nice handwriting" or "what lovely singing voice you have."

- Praise and celebrate effort rather than just achieving goals. If your child cannot complete a specific task, it is just as important to praise him for his effort.

- Be sincere with your praise. Children are rapid to sense when you are not honest. For example, if your child fails to finish a task, you can say something like, "I'm a little disappointed but thank you for trying hard. I know you did your best."
- Never praise your child by comparing him to others. For example, don't say, "You're getting better and better at math. Soon, you'll be as good as your brother." Praise him on his effort and his unique qualities. Do not subconsciously set standards by making comparisons to others.

5 Collaboration

Collaborate with your child in setting rules and tasks. Involving your child in this process and keeping an open communication channel will encourage and incentivize him further.

- Encourage your child to come to you for help.
- Collaborate in solving problems together. Pick a specific problem area and work on it together. For example, if your child misplaces or loses things, exchange suggestions to solve the problem and implement them together. Let him help you choose a special drawer for school things and arrange his school supplies neatly. Place colored baskets in his room to organize his belongings and so on.

The goal of the 5 Cs is to provide your child with the best opportunities to develop and improve his skills in a safe and encouraging environment.

Guidelines for the Family Setting

The best home setting for your child starts with his room. These simple tips can help your child focus better, be more organized and less hyperactive, and moody.

Your child's room

- Keep distractions and clutter to a minimum. Too many toys, posters, and other items will only distract your child and cause him to be more disorganized. Instead, keep only the toys and objects he loves most and store the rest. Interchange toys regularly if your child gets bored but always give him a choice of four or five that he can have in his room at one time.

- Any artwork in your child's room should be serene and soothing to look at. Therefore, posters and artwork should be limited to avoid distractions. Artwork should also be in soft colors and not too bright. Nature and ocean scenes are good choices; however, if your child is old enough to make his own choices, allow him to have the artwork he prefers; just limit the number of posters to two or three.

- Provide reasonable storage solutions to help keep your child organized. Consider color-coded boxes, baskets, shelves, and hooks or plastic containers for small items,

Consider an ADHD-friendly home

- Create a unique work area for your child to do his homework. This area should be away from any background noise to minimize distractions. Experts suggest that the work table should be facing a blank wall and that the child has enough space to move.

- Keep a small basket or cupboard near the door for what your child needs to take with him as he is going out, such as a school bag, books, skates, scarf and hat, and so on. This will avoid the stress of running around and looking for things at the last minute.

- Arrange your home in the style of open spaces and avoid having too many knick-knacks. Of course, all of this makes for easier house cleaning as well!
- If your child's hyperactivity makes him prone to accidents, do not keep breakable things within reach, as he knocks them over and breaks them. Make sure your home is safe and clutter-free.

You are keeping your child's day structured

Your child's day needs to be structured from when he wakes up until he goes to bed. As you have no control over the school setting, this means a morning home and an after-school home routine.

- A set morning routine for breakfast, washing, and dressing help your child set off for school without difficulty or stress.
- Set times for meals when the family eats together.
- Homework should be done at fixed times and in the same place.
- Schedule a fun activity that your child enjoys doing to allow him to unwind before going to bed.
- Do not change schedules and routines often, as this will disorient the child.

Make your child responsible for keeping his room and workspace neat and tidy.

Chapter 8:
Parent Training

The parent training allows parents of children with ADHD to learn strategies to reduce problematic behaviors and improve his relational mode. Parent training is a psychological journey where parents learn effective educational strategies to reduce he behaviors of children with ADHD and improve relational mode, becoming active participants in treating the disorder.

Parent training is a psychological intervention that gives parents the tools to be used for effective behavior management of their children. The term, parent training, is an expression that suggests how this program focuses on enhancing parenting skills within the parent-child relationship. It is a space where parents can practice understanding their child's behavior and employing constructive attitudes while learning to structure an environment that favors self-regulation, autonomy, and reflexivity.

The primary objective is to provide functional behavioral strategies to help parents manage their child's behavior and their own as an educating adult to improve the educational and emotional quality in their relationships with their children. As a result, parents acquire new skills and relational, academic styles as the basis of a parenting style oriented towards problem-solving.

The parent training path was introduced in the late 1960s, starting from the work of Constance Hanf, a clinician interested in modifying aggressive, oppositional, and deviant behaviors of children and young people. Hanf based her work on the importance of parental intervention, recognizing the family as a fundamental resource to foster positive behaviors in the child. This intervention effectively manages children and adolescents with behavioral disorders, especially Attention-Deficit / Hyperactivity Disorder, also known as ADHD. In these cases, common sense and willpower are often not enough: in fact, it is necessary to be aware and adequately know the problems of one's child to put into practice effective behavioral strategies to achieve specific goals and reduce negative behaviors increase positive ones.

In addition, parents who are more reflexive, organized, and coherent in their requests and actions allow their children to develop greater autonomy in finding alternate thoughts and behaviors. This does not mean that families with children with ADHD must have an extremely rigid and rule-filled lifestyle. On the contrary, it is valuable and practical to create a structured environment that gives the child space and time to reflect on what is happening.

The first parent training interventions with parents of children with ADHD date back to the early 1980s, in the light of research and studies that highlighted the conflicting nature of parent-child relationships and interactions in the case of a child with ADHD: especially in situations with many requests from parents, it has been seen that children with ADHD are less adherent and cooperative to the indications and rules imposed on them by their parents, or they are for a shorter time, and show more oppositional and non-complacent attitudes than their peers.

Despite numerous studies on the subject, the clinicians who owe most to the development and use of this approach in ADHD are Russel

Barkley, Karen Wells, and colleagues. Starting from Hanf's model, Barkley defined an intervention path specifically for parents of children with ADHD, consisting of 8 to 10 meetings with a specialized professional; Wells and colleagues instead developed a more extensive and intense parent training program of 27 sessions, with an intervention focused not only on parents but also on the school environment.

With this in mind, the idea of a multimodal approach in treating ADHD acquires more and more value. Today, it is the most effective intervention in the therapy of this disorder, implying the involvement of the family, the school, and the child itself on a path that sees the combination of behavioral therapies, clinical-psychological interventions, and drug therapies based on the severity of the disorder.

How does parent training work?

The parent training program generally provides for the holding of 8-12 weekly meetings between parents of children and adolescents with ADHD with a specifically trained trainer, in most cases a psychologist. The interval between one session and another is specially designed to give families space and time to implement the information, advice, and strategies learned in the various meetings and reflect, in subsequent sessions, on the difficulties encountered and the results obtained. All meetings aim to gather information regarding situations in which your child uses inappropriate behavior and prepares parents for a change.

Step 1: Information and investigation of the disorder

The trainer describes the specific characteristics of the disorder, illustrating its causes, course, possible risk behaviors, effective and ineffective treatments. Both the most common and best-known elements are dealt with in detail, such as impulsivity and inattention. Parents are usually less aware, such as frustration, anger, shame, feeling "different" or "wrong". In the first place, this initial moment allows to inform parents correctly and comprehensively about the disorder and its nature and increase their awareness of it; second, greater cognition will enable them to understand better their children's mood, emotions, and behavior.

Step 2: Understand the parent-child relationship

In this session, parents learn about the causes of their children's harmful and disruptive behaviors and identify them within their family environment, sharing and discussing previously experienced episodes with the group. The trainer instructs participants in the antecedent-behavior-consequence model to recognize and remember the events potentially triggering negative behavior and explains the four factors involved in developing problem behaviors in children: the characteristics of the child, aspects of the parents, stressful events in the family environment, and parenting style.

Step 3: Enhance Positive Interactions

The trainer's task in this meeting is to convey to parents the importance of relating positively with their children, especially during the manifestation of negative behavior. They are involved and invited to discuss this competence, practice, and practice with the group and share their experiences.

Step 4: Extend Positive Interactions and Increase Children's Complacency

In this phase, parents are urged to notice and highlight their children's positive behaviors when they find themselves in difficult situations, giving them immediate and consistent positive reinforcements. Strategies are then illustrated for issuing commands and rules most effectively: making direct, short requests with achievable and short-term objectives.

Step 5: Use points or coin system at home

Parents learn the token economy system, a rewards system that reinforces the child's appropriate behaviors to encourage more excellent attendance in the future. Parents will be asked to draw up a list of rewards and support that can motivate the child and the second list of those behaviors and rules they would like the child to abide by, while being given a score or tokens when enacted. The points or tokens earned will provide the child the opportunity to reach the final prize. Token economy objectives and rewards can be shared and decided with your child to make him feel more involved and responsible in this intervention.

Step 6: Include 'Sanctions'

When inappropriate behavior occurs, the token economy provides for the use of penalties, which consist of subtracting previously earned points or tokens. At the beginning of the program, the parent shares the behaviors that will cause him to lose points with the child.

Step 7: Use Time Out

If severe negative behaviors occur, parents are instructed in the time out technique, which requires the child to retire for a few minutes (one for each year of age) in tranquility in a space that allows him to get away from the non-functional behavior committed, to process it and calm down. Before starting, parents discuss and agree with their child the reasons that trigger the time out and the number of warnings that the parent will give to the child before using it. At the end of the time out, the child goes back to his activity.

Step 8: Regulate behavior in public places

In this phase, parents learn to extend the program even outside the home environment, with some precautions to be applied based on the external context. First, the trainer identifies with the parents, who will share with their child the places where they manifest non-functional behaviors.

Step 9: Problematic behaviors in school and preparation at the end of the program

Parents learn to use the prize system at school, supporting constant feedback from the child's teachers regarding functional and non-functional behaviors previously shared with him. To achieve this goal, a collaboration between parents and teachers is essential, which requires periodic sharing of the problem behaviors highlighted and strategies to learn how to manage them in the best possible way.

Step 10: Follow-up

This is a control session at the end of the path, in which parents and Trainer discuss the changes obtained, any resistance still present, and how to manage them.

Why take a Parent Training Course

Taking care of children with ADHD can generate intense, stressful situations in parents, with the risk of repercussions on relationships within the family and, consequently, on the disorder's symptoms.

Families of children with ADHD are often characterized by less "emotional warmth". Parents experience poor parental competence and poverty of effective educational strategies, leading to guilt, frustration, and anger.

An important aspect that emerges from multiple studies in this field is the positive correlation between functional relationships and educational coherence within the family and less severe symptomatology of the disorder, greater social acceptance, and more meaningful social skills. The family is, therefore, a fundamental resource to draw upon for the treatment of ADHD; based on this, parent training aims to modify those relationships that are dysfunctional, providing parents with valuable tools to bring out the educational potential that each possesses but they sometimes struggle to implement.

Finally, this path offers parents an opportunity to share and compare their experiences and emotions: a space in which they realize they are not alone, in which they discover new sides and ways of being for their children and rediscover others, and at which they now look with fresh eyes.

Chapter 9:
Parenting Strategies for Kids with ADHD

W hen a child gets diagnosed with ADHD, parenting goes to a whole new level. Regular tasks can turn into struggles. Your life can become chaotic if you let your feelings, especially your frustrations, show a negative impact on your daily routine. Most parents are undoubtedly correct. But to be a parent to a child or teenager who has ADHD, you have to be more than just good.

Don't despair! It's not an easy job, it's hard, but you can make things a little easier for you and your child with the following tips and strategies.

Acceptance is Key to a Better Life with Your Child

It's a given that your child gets loved by everyone in the family. But accepting him and his situation is an entirely different thing. Parents and other family members should not make him feel resentment towards his disorder (not necessarily your child), which puts him at risk for low self-esteem. Don't negatively think of his inexhaustible energy. One parent whose child has ADHD says she's even jealous of his enthusiasm and can think of unusual careers he can have in the future.

Stay Calm and Focused

Dealing with children whose anger escalates quickly can indeed be very frustrating. But just like every day parenting, showing an agitated child that you're spiraling out of control has a negative impact. Instead of "intimidating him to stop what he's doing," the results can backfire. So watch yourself closely, especially if your initial reaction is to react negatively.

Take note that trying to reason out with your child will only have adverse effects. While doing his homework, for example, he'll be making a lot of fuss. By arguing with your child and telling him to "stop complaining," you'll only be setting yourself up for a trap. Preparation time will extend, and when you're pressed for time to do other chores, anger can escalate rather quickly. To diffuse the situation, acknowledge his frustration and give him a gentle touch. Avoid yelling at him or even chastising him for "dawdling."

Control Yourself and Be a Good Role Model

As parents, you are naturally your child's influential role models. Children will follow anything you say or do. Keep yourself in check, especially if you're angry. Yelling at your child makes him think that it's okay to do the same thing as well. The need to exercise self-control is crucial, especially in this situation. You can't expect your child to be calm when he sees you out of control as well.

Most parents think that being loud can intimidate their children. Understandably, you can't avoid being angry at your child, but you can certainly stop shouting at him continually.

The second time you're angry, take a few deep breaths or leave the room. If you have techniques that help soothe you when you're mad at work, use them. Showing the importance of self-control makes it easier to help them manage their emotions as well.

Help Your Child, But Set Limits

We always want to rescue our children whenever they're in a rush. But, unfortunately, it can harm their independence. The more you do things for your children, the more they will rely on you and the less they'll do for themselves.

Be supportive, but let your child do specific tasks by himself. For instance, when it comes to homework, encourage him to work on it without your help. If you have to monitor him, then don't hover. Instead, sit near him, and work on your own. It is an excellent time to tackle unfinished reports, update your blog and the like.

Don't Underestimate Your Child

You get hurt when the staff at school labels him as a slow learner. Sometimes, out of frustration, you might just believe it. You shouldn't. After all, a child with ADHD is not necessarily a slow learner. His mind just doesn't work like the other children's. He can still be successful if you give him a little challenge. Those negative remarks might push you to pull him out of school and teach him yourself. But it would help if you stopped yourself from doing that.

One thing you can do is find an appropriate school for him. A public school might not be the best solution, and maybe a school for children with special needs won't do him any good either. Instead, aim for schools that have higher expectations, a place where he gets challenged positively.

Additionally, introduce your child to the power of making sound choices. Besides preparing him to be self-reliant, he exercises control when he gets a chance to make a wise decision. A technique that works well in such circumstances is well known as "structured choice."

For example: you may ask, "Do you want to work on math questions or your science assignment first?" or "We need to put your toys back before we go out. Do you want to pick them up from the floor first, or start with the ones on your bed?"

Know the Difference Between Discipline and Punishment

Most parents would not know the difference. To discipline a child, explain what would happen if they break a rule and the rewards they can get if they continue to be on their best behavior. Explaining to them about inappropriate behavior is discipline. Avoid yelling, threatening, taking away toys, and spanking if you haven't presented anything to him.

That's not discipline! That's verbal and physical abuse and will not work at all. Likewise, the punishment that uses fear to make your child listen to you does not work.

Focus on Teamwork with Your Child

Just as you would work things out with your spouse or co-workers to agree, you should be doing the same thing with your child. Of course, it's natural to expect him to break some rules, the same thing that other children will do. But remember, you're not perfect, and neither is your child. When it comes to facing negative behavior consequences, work with your child to avoid such a situation.

You might say: "What will Mommy do if you won't put your toys back after playing with them?" He will respond with a "punishment" he deems appropriate for his bad behavior (i.e., five minutes' time-out). In that way, he won't feel that you're punishing him. Instead, he'll be able to recognize what he did wrong and submit himself to the consequences.

You should also set up "mini rewards" for his excellent behavior. For example, in this simple way, if he picks up his toys after playing with them without being told to do so, reward him with an extra hour of playing video games.

Separate the Disorder from the Child

You should remember that he's not precisely defiant just because "he wants to." Take note that with ADHD, being distracted or inattentive is one of the symptoms. So when you tell your child to fix his bed and find him in front of the computer with the bed unmade, remind him about your request.

It's incredibly frustrating if you have to repeat what you said several times, but you shouldn't resort to calling him lazy, a slob, space, or other negative words you can think of. Avoid screaming about picking up his toys because he won't listen and even stop yelling about his assignment mistakes.

Instead, use the teamwork technique to solve a problem. For example, "We have a problem with your toys, and I need your help to solve it."

Research More about ADHD

Parents need to understand their children's behavior to help them fight the battle. That's why there is a variety of support groups for parents who have children with ADHD. Aside from that, there's an influx of reliable sources on the Internet to help you figure out your child.

Knowledge is power! When you know more, you'll find out that you're able to handle the situation better. In addition, you can anticipate problems that might lead to potentially harmful behavior.

Anticipate and Avoid Problems

Go over the rules before you go inside a grocery store or anywhere public. Make sure to talk to them about plans as well. For example: if you're at a party and you're starting to realize that there's a potential problem that's about to explode, ask to speak to him calmly. You may take him from the group or leave earlier (depending on what you agreed on).

Take Care of Yourself

Ask for help from family members and close friends when you need some time off. You must have alone time to help you manage the stress.

Find ways to help reduce stress:

- Reading books
- Watching a movie

Your health is important; getting enough rest, eating the right food, and exercising keep you healthy and strong. Best of all, cut yourself some slack and understand that you are not a magician, nobody's perfect, and know the value of a reliable support system.

Chapter 10:
The Wining Strategies of Parenting a Child with ADHD

A s a parent, your role is to set the stage for your child's physical, mental, and emotional health. You can control the many aspects that positively impact the symptoms of your child's disorder. Keep in mind that these principles require continuous reinforcement. In addition, this parenting method necessitates that you pause when your child has made a transgression, and then you can take the time to reflect on the strategies discussed in this book and use that delay to choose a response that aligns with these strategies.

1. Give Immediate feedback and apply consequences

So if you want the child to focus on the job at hand, you need to use positive feedback. State and apply clear consequences that define the rewards they will get if they complete it and the mild punishment they will be confronted with if they don't. The same goes for when you're trying to change negative behavior.

You have to provide swift positive feedback for good behavior and immediate negative consequences for inappropriate actions. Positive feedback includes giving praise and compliments. Keep in mind that you need to openly and specifically articulate what your child did that was positive. With that said, credit by itself might not be sufficient in motivating your child to stick with the task at hand. So it's recommended that you set up a point system that grants your child special rewards and extra privileges when they accumulate a certain number of points. When you provide feedback, make sure it's immediate to help change your child's behavior more efficiently.

2. Give feedback more frequently

Your child needs feedback that is not just quick and immediate but also frequent. While swift consequences and feedback can be beneficial when given occasionally, they're far more helpful when provided more often. While this can become a bit frustrating and invasive to your child and exhausting for you, especially if you go too far with it, it's necessary, especially if you're trying to change a specific pattern of misbehavior on their part.

3. Use more compelling reinforcements

A child with ADHD needs more powerful and compelling reinforcements than other children, particularly when they're asked to behave, follow the rules, and perform tasks. These reinforcements include, but are not limited to: privileges, snacks, treats, points, physical affection, toys, and even money (though only occasionally).

Admittedly, not all children should be frequently rewarded with material things because that can compromise intrinsic rewards like the desire to make their loved ones happy or the pride of learning a new skill. However, inherent tips are far less likely to incite children with ADHD to change their behavior.

4. Opt for encouragement before punishment

Most parents use some form of punishment to discipline their children when they misbehave or disobey. This can be effective for children without ADHD because their transgressions are not a regular occurrence. However, for a child with ADHD that is susceptible to misbehaving more frequently, recurring punishment will result in a great deal of negativity.

Research suggests that children with this disability are already being punished significantly more often than their typical counterparts. So beginning your behavioral control plan with even more punishment is not a sustainable strategy, not to mention that it's also unlikely to work.

5. Establish a structure to simplify completing tasks

Help your child stay focused and organized with the following tips:

- Create and sustain a routine
- Use clocks and timers
- Simplify your child's schedule
- Create a quiet environment

6. Place physical reminders of important information

The ability to store the pertinent information to complete a given task is impaired in children with ADHD. In addition, because their working memory is deficient compared to other children, they need constant reminders of vital information to help them stay on track and maintain their focus. To remedy this, you should turn that information into a physical form, so it's more accessible to the child when they're performing their tasks. For example, take a piece of paper or a card and make a list of essential rules your child should follow while working, reminders such as "stay on track," "don't zone out," "read instructions carefully," "double-check your answers to make sure they're complete," "ask for help if you need it," etc.

7. Provide external incentives and motivation boosts

Children with ADHD have a hard time processing mental information and references of time and preparations for the future, but they also struggle with self-motivation. They cannot channel their inner motivation to follow through with tasks they find tedious, boring, arduous, or lengthy. This deficit in self-motivation can be surmounted to a significant degree using external motivation boosts in the form of incentives, rewards, and positive feedback.

These incentives will push the child to behave themselves, follow the rules, or restrict their activity based on what is needed of them now. The goal here is to create a win/win situation where your child gets something they want by following instructions, and you get what you want, which is them being obedient and compliant.

8. Externalize thinking and problem-solving

A child with ADHD does not work with or manipulate mental information in the same way. They have a hard time stopping to think about the problem or situation at hand, and they tend to respond impulsively without any proper consideration of the options in front of them. So it might be more fruitful for you as a parent to find ways to externalize thinking and problem-solving (much like providing physical reminders of time and important information).

9. Be consistent in your efforts.

The goal here should be to strive for consistency in your efforts to apply these strategies and guidelines. This means being consistent over time, being determined, and not giving up at the first sign of trouble, especially when you're attempting to change a behavior, using the same responses to build predictability, even if the setting changes, and making sure that both you and your partner are united in your efforts.

If your methods are unpredictable and erratic, this only opens up the door to failure and confusion. The same goes for giving up too soon when you're trying to enforce or eliminate a pattern of behavior. You should try a strategy for one to two weeks before pulling the plug and deciding that it is ineffective.

10. Plan in anticipation of bad situations

As a parent, you have the experience and the ability to safely predict settings in which your child is inclined to misbehave or disobey the rules. So leverage that information and use it to reinforce feedback and consequences. For example, if you're aware that your child tends to go wild and wreak havoc when you're at a family member's or friend's house, use this in preparation for these problems and when they occur.

Anticipation can save you so much anguish and frustration further down the line. So next time you find yourself about to enter a setting that triggers your child's misbehavior or symptoms, develop a plan of action and share it with them in advance. Moreover, make sure you follow through with that plan of action should problems come to the surface. Just sharing those rules and instructions with your child can significantly reduce the severity of their actions.

Before you go into a store, restaurant, mall, or other public settings, pause for a moment and review the basic instructions they are expected to follow with your child. These could be simple statements that are straight to the point, so along the lines of "no running around," "stay next to me," "no shouting or yelling," and "do as I tell you."

As you clearly state these rules, ask your child to repeat them after you, then set up the incentive. This could be getting to pick out an item of their choice at the store, for instance, or some other privilege. In addition, you also need to explain the punishment if they don't obey those rules. Remember that whatever happens, you follow the plan and provide immediate and frequent feedback while you're there. If you must, then punishment should be swift in response to their violation of the rules.

11. Keep their disorder in perspective.

Managing a difficult child with ADHD can be a daunting challenge. At times, you will find yourself angry, frustrated, embarrassed, or at the very least disheartened when your attempts at parenting seem to be going down the drain. This can even cause you to lose all perspective as you're confronted with endless and aimless arguments that lead nowhere.

But it's at these very moments that you need to remember you are the parent, the adult in this situation, and above all, you are that disabled child's teacher and mentor. If either of you has to be the calm and composed one, then it is you.

A great way to keep your cool in challenging instances is to distance yourself from your child's behavior and symptoms. You can do that by mentally removing yourself from that environment. Focus on your breathing, count to ten, think of someplace you'd rather be, then reevaluate the situation from a different perspective.

12. Don't take things personally

Whichever strategy or principle you are seeking to implement, do not take things personally. Don't let your sense of self-worth get entangled in your ability to "win" some argument or other with your child. Nobody is keeping score, and your dignity is not on the line if you 'lose' at an encounter or discussion.

Always strive to stay as calm as possible, maintain a sense of humor if you can, and use the strategies to guide the exchanges you have with your child. Sometimes, this may entail leaving the premises to clear your head and get back to your senses, and that's completely normal.

It's no failure on your part, so don't assume you're a terrible parent simply because you can't get your kid to comply. All parents fail at regulating their children's behavior occasionally; so don't beat yourself up for that but instead learn to practice forgiveness and let go of your anger and disappointment. What is more important in this case is to focus on getting it done better the next time.

Chapter 11:
Methods for Living with an ADHD Child

B y this point, you have taken in a lot of ADHD information. You know what it is and all of the available treatment options for your child. You now know that he does not have to suffer from ADHD in vain. The disorder can be managed—your child will be able to live with ADHD. While you have also learned of the available help to you as the parent of an ADHD child, day-to-day life can be difficult. Knowing how to live with an ADHD child is vital in treating his disorder, and it will make life that much easier for you as his parent. There are various methods you can use at home to aid in ADHD treatment.

Parental Tips and Tools

Being the parent of an ADHD child requires patience and understanding more than anything else. Your child is sure to push you to your limits on different occasions. The various ADHD behaviors can be frustrating for you. Behavior management goes beyond the therapy sessions with your ADHD child. Managing the behaviors at home can be challenging, but it is doable. These tips and tools will help you manage and cope with ADHD at home.

- **Acceptance** – You have to accept that your child has ADHD. This means that he is not exactly like other children or even his siblings. Acceptance is essential to your child because he needs to know that he is loved, no matter what. However, the quicker you accept the diagnosis, the faster you can start modifying behaviors with your child.

- **Rules** – At home, you have to define the rules clearly. With an ADHD child, you cannot simply say that running is not allowed. Words are likely to go in one ear and out the other. Your child needs clear, precise rules. The best thing to do is write them down and display the rules in a prominent place in the house.

- **Be consistent** – As mentioned, consistency is the key to modifying behaviors. You must follow through on both rewards and consequences. ADHD children need consistency in their lives. They need to know that when a parent says something, it will happen. Failing to follow through is only going to make your ADHD child not trust your word. He is more likely to push those boundaries to see how far he can go.

- **Routines** – ADHD children thrive with routine schedules. You must establish a way for your child that you can both adhere to every day. These daily routines do not necessarily have to be the same. For instance, weekday routines and weekend routines can differ. The important thing is that you follow these routines every day and every week. Practices become habits, and you want your ADHD child to establish good practices. Prepare a written schedule your child can look at whenever he needs a reminder about what he should be doing or what is coming.

- **Immediate rewards and consequences** – When managing ADHD at home, you have to give a direct response to your child's behaviors. You cannot wait to provide him with a result because he may not even remember what happened later. The same is true for rewards. He needs to know right away when he does something positive or something negative. The immediate reactions will begin to mold his behaviors at home.

- **Be positive** – As a parent, you need to look at each situation with a positive attitude. Even wrong concerns should be dealt with in a supportive manner. Your ADHD child needs encouragement for even the little things. Positivity will help your child have better self-esteem and build confidence. Just make sure that you are not putting too much pressure on your child by being positive about everything. You can support him when he has a behavioral mishap without making him feel like it is okay to behave negatively.

- **Be flexible** – Yes, your child needs rules and structure, and routine. He will thrive with a schedule. However, this is an ADHD child you live with, and you simply must allow room for flexibility. There is no guarantee that every rule or routine will always be followed without problems. Prepare for the unexpected so that when it happens, you are ready. Remember: you are not perfect, and you should not expect perfection from your ADHD child.

- **Stay Organized** – Lack of organization will only slow down your child's progress. He is easily distracted and forgetful. Therefore, he needs his living space organized in a way that enhances his life. One thing you can do is manage his bedroom. Use baskets with labels to make sure he knows where all of his things belong. Create a quiet place for homework that is free from distractions. Think of it like this: your ADHD child's mind is already in an almost constant state of disarray and disorder. A peaceful, organized environment at home can help calm his mind.

- **Cut down on screen time** – Children enjoy gaming and television. So why not play board games with the family? Try to keep your child active and engaged to prevent boredom. Do not let cable television become a babysitter for your child. Sure, it might give you a few moments of peace, but is it helping your ADHD child? Instead, consider using screen time as a part of positive reinforcement. For example, your child can earn extra time on his favorite video game by achieving weekly goals.

- **Interaction** – Another vital tool for living with an ADHD child is to interact with him. Talk to your child. Listen to his thoughts and ideas. Ask him about his day at school. No child, with ADHD or not, likes to feel ignored by their loved ones. So make time every day to interact one-on-one with your child.

- **Sleep routines** – So many ADHD children have trouble sleeping. Since sleep is the body's way of healing and recharging for the next day, it is obvious why it is so important. A calming lavender bath before bedtime is relaxing. Follow the routine each night to help your child establish a sleep pattern that lets him get the rest he needs.

- **Learn how to say yes** – It is easy for all parents to fall into the habit of always saying no to a child's request. Make an effort to start saying yes to reasonable requests. If your ADHD child always hears you telling him no, he is more likely to rebel. Listen to your child's demands and pay attention. For instance, is a late-night snack going to cause some sort of problem for your child? Even when you have to say no, talk about your decision with your child. Explain why you are saying no instead of just expecting him to accept it.

- **Be prepared** – Do not expect your child to behave all of the time. It simply is not going to happen, especially with an ADHD child. Before you and your child go to the store or visit a friend, sit him down and make a plan. Discuss your expectations for his behavior during the outing and discuss the consequences and rewards. Your ADHD child always needs to know what he can expect. Learn to see the signs of when your child is about to have a meltdown. It is always easier to stop it before it gets started.

Taking Care of the Parent

All of this time, we have focused on what you can do for your ADHD child. But you are only human; you have to incorporate self-care into your life, too. Living with an ADHD child is not easy. You are going to be pushed to your limits. You are going to feel overwhelmed and frustrated. You are likely to lose your temper. Just as you need to know when your child is about to lose control, you must recognize those signs within yourself. The following tips will help you take the best care of yourself to take the best care of your child.

- Take a break when you feel yourself reaching your limits. This is essentially giving yourself a time-out. Parents get stressed and overwhelmed, too, especially when dealing with ADHD. Do not let ADHD control every aspect of your life. Instead, walk away from a challenging situation and give yourself time to calm down. When you are calm, you can return to the problem with a clear head and better determine how to handle it.

- To get calm, try meditation or even the "count to ten" method. Deep breathing and other relaxation techniques will help you get back in control of your own emotions. Remember that your ADHD child is watching you. He needs to see that even you, the parent, get frustrated. He needs to know how you deal with emotions, and he can even learn how to calm himself with you.

  Come up with a code word that puts the situation or argument on hold while the two of you get centered and refocused. If he is on the verge of an outburst, and you can feel your nerves reaching their limit, use the code word to signal to hit the pause button while both of you use relaxation and calming techniques to regain control of emotions. Then, both of you will come back to the scenario with a calm, clear mind.

- Ask for help when you need it. You need time for yourself. Do not be afraid to make that time for yourself by enlisting the use of your family or even a babysitter.

- Utilize therapy options for yourself. Talking over ADHD issues with a professional can be quite helpful in reducing stress. A professional can give you proven advice and techniques to use at home. Even venting to a friend can help. While your friend may not have a helpful suggestion for you, getting things off your chest can be a perfect stress reliever. You do not need to keep your thoughts and feelings bottled up inside. Instead, find a safe environment to let them out.

A happy, healthy parent is vital to treating ADHD and living with the accompanying behaviors. Make time every week just for you. Go ahead and take that long bubble bath. The better you are, the better your child is likely to be.

Chapter 12:
Managing ADHD Behaviors

N ow let's get into what living at home with your daughter with ADHD looks like. We will cover some of the challenging moments, such as bedtime, mealtime, and playdates, and then we will start to look at supporting your daughter at school. .

Managing Life at Home

Homelife can be challenging for a girl with ADHD. The most challenging moments can include times of transition (mealtimes and bedtimes); managing issues that come up with your daughter socially, such as friendships and playdates, can be equally tricky. So I'm going to offer you some tips and strategies to help you keep these times as peaceful as possible.

Bed Time

Younger children with ADHD may have difficulty winding down and resist going to bed because it feels uncomfortable. I have a few tips that can help:

- **Have a consistent, mutually agreed-upon bedtime.** This is key to reducing arguments and resistance about the actual time. Pick a time that is realistic for both your daughter and your family. Use a visual schedule reminder or a timer to help your daughter know when bedtime is approaching.
- **Create a calming bedtime routine.** Encourage your daughter to engage in quiet activities, such as reading, drawing, yoga, journaling, listening to music, or audiobooks.

These cues can help induce sleepiness for children who struggle with sleep issues. If possible, eliminate screen time at least 30 minutes before bed.

- **Be flexible.** Sometimes it's okay to bend the rules a little bit. For example, allowing some flexibility for busy nights when everyone is stretched is fine, and it teaches your daughter to turn a little as well.

Mealtimes

Family meals are supposed to be the time for everyone to come together and catch up on their day, but they can be difficult for kids who have a hard time staying seated.

- **Make the conversation fun by playing games.** Have a stack of silly questions to ask one another over dinner.
- **Recruit a helper.** Many girls with ADHD enjoy independence and the satisfaction of helping with chores. Enlist your daughter's help with cooking, setting the table, or selecting the music.
- **Keep it short.** Some kids have a hard time staying seated, so expecting them to sit for 30 minutes for a meal is just not realistic. Instead, give yourself permission to have shorter meals and excuse your child when she finishes if she can no longer be a productive part of the mealtime.

Playdates

Playdates can be tricky for younger children with ADHD. The truth is that all children benefit from learning how to socialize in less structured environments. There are a few ways to help ensure your daughter has a successful playdate:

- **Practice play planning with your daughter.** Before your daughter has a playdate, discuss with her what she would like to play and various scenarios that could take place. Help her foresee problems by asking questions like, "I wonder if we should put your American Girl doll away since you have only one and it might be hard to share. What do you think?"

- **Keep the playdate shorter.** Start with scheduling shorter playdates. For example, have your daughter invite a friend over for an hour. Allow them to do an activity, have a snack, and then be done. Having shorter, successful playdates can help build everyone's confidence levels. As your daughter begins to get the hang of it, you can slowly increase the length of the playdate.

- **Model problem-solving.** If your daughter encounters an issue on the playdate, you may be inclined to end it immediately, but use the opportunity to help her develop her problem-solving skills. For example, if your daughter insists on choosing the movie to watch, ask her to come up with a list of three movies and let her friend choose from that list.

Managing Life at School

For some families, managing school and all that comes with it can be the most challenging endeavor.

Advocating for Your Daughter

You are the expert on your daughter, which makes you her best advocate. Ensure to reach out at the beginning of the academic year and let your daughter's teacher know what has worked for her in other classroom settings, what motivates her, and what she finds challenging. In addition, ask your daughter's teacher how you can best support them. Establishing these lines of communication early on will help you and your daughter's teacher by members of the same team.

Accommodations to Request

Accommodations are changes in education made to remove learning barriers. They are given to those with disabilities or special needs in school.

IEP/504

Accommodations can usually be made via two routes: either the Individuals with Disabilities Education Act (IDEA) or Section 504 of the Rehabilitation Act. Depending on which course best meets your daughter's needs, she will either have an IEP (individualized education plan) or a 504 plan. Both require a special meeting with specific members of your daughter's school, such as her teacher, school psychologist, speech therapist, occupational therapist, or a learning disability teaching consultant.

Study partner/peer tutoring: Pairing your daughter with a positive peer-study role model can help her learn new study habits. Make sure it's someone with whom she has a good rapport. If your daughter is older, ask her teachers for suggestions of students who may be good study partners outside of school.

Quiet workspaces/alternative test settings: Some children with ADHD benefit greatly from taking tests or doing focus-intensive work in an alternative environment, such as a cubicle or quiet library; they may even benefit from using noise-canceling headphones to minimize distractions. Explore with your child's teacher whether your child might help from this accommodation.

Breaking down assignments: Large assignments, such as papers, projects, and book reports, can overwhelm all children. Kids with ADHD, in particular, may struggle with where to start sequentially and how to break down the assignment into realistic goals. Having more significant lessons organized into smaller, digestible pieces can make the work much more attainable and accessible.

Movement breaks: Movement breaks, or sensory breaks, can be incredibly helpful, especially for children who struggle with staying seated. A knowledgeable teacher will know how to incorporate movement breaks in more discreet ways (such as assigning short tasks or chores), which allow for movement but are not discriminatory.

Color-coding: Studies show that using color-coded systems can help kids with ADHD make better associations; they may also help with organizing and timekeeping. Encourage your child to color-code folders and notebooks for different classes or subjects. Later, when you write down assignments, you can keep the colors consistent using similarly colored highlighters and pens (or fonts, if your daughter keeps a digital calendar or planner).

Assistive technology: Many schools offer technology-based educational tools to help children with ADHD manage their symptoms and co-occurring learning issues. Some standard tools include transcription software, which allows a child to dictate ideas onto a computer document; audiobook library access; and C-Pens, which can highlight short pieces of text (such as homework) and read it aloud to a child.

How to Deal with Social Media

Social media adds an extra layer of complication for adolescent girls, as well as their parents. Not only do girls have to be conscious of their face-to-face interactions, but there is also an awareness of a constant conversation and commentary happening via text and social media apps (such as Instagram, Snapchat, and TikTok). In addition, many parents have never dealt with social media before, and it can create several issues.

While some girls can separate themselves from what's happening online, others have a challenging time with it. Therefore, it's essential to talk to your daughter openly as soon as she gets her first smartphone or device that allows her to communicate via text and social media. The crucial conversations should center around etiquette, dealing with online bullying, and sending and receiving pictures.

I once heard a parent ask a police officer, who was providing a parents' focused social media training, how old their child should be when they give them their first phone. He answered, when you feel comfortable with your child viewing pornography. This may sound harsh, but it is the reality. Once your child has access to texting, the Internet, and social media, they'll be able to find things they aren't ready to see. It's up to you to put in safeguards, whether it's apps to monitor their activity, limiting their time and access, or having periodic phone checks.

ADHD and Puberty

As your daughter starts to move into puberty, her brain will undergo many changes. Hormonally, the increase of estrogen can directly affect the levels of norepinephrine and dopamine in the brain. Due to this hormonal increase, it's not uncommon for a girl's ADHD symptoms to increase during puberty. This becomes especially apparent during menstruation when hormonal levels are at their peak. You can help your daughter better prepare for these changes by helping her track her menstrual cycle.

Chapter 13:
Discipline a Child with ADHD?

C hildren with ADHD frequently need a slightly different way of coping. A few straightforward adjustments to your parenting approaches could provide your child with the tools to control his behavior more efficiently. By definition, children with ADHD may have difficulty sitting still, finishing tasks, handling impulses, and subsequent instructions. These field strategies can help assist children with ADHD obey the principles.

1. Give favorable attention

Parenting a child with ADHD may be exhausting. Their endless source of energy and urge to speak always can tire even the most patient parent. Good playtime reduces attention-seeking behavior. Plus, it'll make your consequences more successful. However, challenging your kid's behavior was, set aside a single time with your child daily. Giving your kid only 15 minutes of clear focus is just one of the most straightforward yet most efficient techniques to decrease behavioral issues.

2. Give powerful instructions

Children with brief attention spans require more help with subsequent instructions. Quite many times, they do not hear the directions properly in the first location. There are numerous things you can do to create your demands longer effective. Gain your kid's complete attention before giving instructions. For example, switch off the tv, establish eye contact, and set a hand on your kid's shoulder before stating, "please wash your room."

Prevent string orders such as "put in your socks, wash your area, and then remove the garbage" will probably get lost in translation. A young child with ADHD is very likely to put his socks in the wash on the way to his room, but he will find something else to do instead of wash them. Give instruction at one time. Then, ask your child to repeat back to you precisely what he learned to ensure that he completely understands.

3. Praise your kid's effort

Catch your child being good and tip out it. Praise motivates children using ADHD to act, and regular feedback is significant. Make your compliments specific. Rather than saying, "fine job," say, "good job placing your dish at the sink when I asked you to," invite children for subsequent instructions, playing gently, and sitting, and you're going to encourage your kid to keep this up.

4. Utilize time-out when needed

Time-out can be a fantastic method to help children with ADHD calm their bodies and their wisdom.2time-out does not have to be a brutal punishment. On the contrary, it is sometimes an excellent life skill that may be helpful in several conditions. Educate your child to go to a quiet place to calm down if he is overstimulated or frustrated. Then, finally, he'll learn how to put himself time-out until he gets into trouble.

5. Ignore mild misbehaviors

Children with ADHD frequently exhibit attention-seeking behavior. Therefore, offering them attention, even if it is negative, supports those behaviors to last. Ignoring moderate misbehaviors educates them that devious behavior will not get the desirable benefits. Ignore complaining, whining, loud sounds, and efforts to disrupt you, and finally, your son or daughter will stop.

6. Establish a bonus system

Reward systems may be a terrific way to help children with ADHD remain on course.1 establish a couple of target behaviors, like staying at the table at a dinner or utilizing gentle touches using a furry friend. Kids with ADHD frequently get bored with conventional reward systems, which need them to wait for too much time to make a reward. So instead, produce a market system that aids your kid in earning tokens through the day. After that, allow tickets to be traded for larger prizes, such as electronic equipment or an opportunity to play a favorite sport together.

7. Permit for natural consequences

When picking out a child with ADHD, choose your battles wisely. Of course, you do not want your kid to feel like he cannot do anything that he is always getting into trouble. But, on the other hand, letting some behaviors will be able to help you maintain your sanity too.

Sometimes, letting for natural effects makes more sense instead of convincing a kid to make a much better decision. For instance, if your son or daughter insists that he does not have to rest from playing to consume lunch, then let him skip dinner. The natural result is that he will likely be starving afterward and will need to wait until dinner. Then, finally, he will learn how to eat lunch in time.

8. Work with your child's behavior

When parents work with a kid's instructor, it increases the likelihood a kid will be prosperous in college. However, some kids need alterations to their college job, for example, being granted additional time on tests to become successful.

Behavior modification s could be necessary also. For example, needing a child with ADHD to keep in for recess can worsen behavior issues. So it is imperative to work with each other to make a behavior management program that will encourage your kid's attempts to handle his symptoms.

A behavior management plan that conveys between school and home can be helpful. For example, a kid may receive components or points out of his instructor who could be traded for rights in your home like watching TV or using a personal computer.

Positive parenting advice for kids with ADHD

Most parents are great buddies. However, if your kid has focus deficit hyperactivity disorder, "great" might be insufficient. Fortunately, it's easier than you might picture to move from good to good ADHD parenting. All it requires is a few tiny alterations to your parenting approaches and how you interact with your kid and respond to their poor behavior. Here is what works...

1. Accept the fact your kid - like most of the kids - is not imperfect

ADHD in kids is ordinary although not always straightforward. It is difficult to accept that there is something unusual about your youngster. However, a kid who feels their parents' bitterness and pessimism for their prospects is not likely to develop the self-esteem and can-do soul to be able to turn into a joyful, well-adjusted mature person. Do your very best to enjoy your child unconditionally. Treat him like he had been currently the individual who you want him to be. That will enable him to become that individual.

2. Do not think of all of the "bad news" about your child's ADHD

It is no pleasure to listen to college workers explain your kid as "slow" or even unmotivated; it isn't adequate to hear just about the awful behavior. But do not let negative opinions dissuade you by doing what in your ability to urge for their instructional needs. In the end, children with ADHD can succeed if they receive the aid they want.

3. Do not underestimate the significance of ADHD medicine

There is no doubt that the ideal ADHD medication produces a massive impact on behavior for most kids. But by no means does this indicate that medicine is the one thing that makes a distinction. Speaking about it will render the child feeling that excellent behavior has to do with her drugs. If you catch your kid doing whatever you've repeatedly requested her not to do, then fight the impulse to ask, "Can you forget to take your medicine this morning?" and do not threaten to lift your kid's dosage since they did something improper.

4. Ensure to understand the difference between punishment and discipline

How frequently have you complained to friends or relatives (as well as a therapist), "I have cried, lectured, jeopardized, awarded time-outs, removed toys, perennial excursions, bribed, cried, and much spanked but nothing works!" Can you find the issue with this strategy? And among the very best methods - the carrot stick - is not even cited.

5. Quit blaming others for your kid's difficulties

Are you the type of parent that finds fault with everybody except their youngster? For example, do you say things such as "that motorist doesn't have any control over the children on the bus, or if the instructor proved better at behavior control, my kid would not have much difficulty in college?"

Other people can bring about a kid's issues. But seeking to pin the blame solely on others motivates your child to choose the easy way out. Why should they accept personal accountability for their activities if they blame somebody else (as they hear you do so)?

Chapter 14:
How to Deal with Children Who Have ADHD

Now that you are equipped with basic information about ADHD and what to expect from your child's behavior, it is time to learn about the proper ways of dealing with your child. Your child is unique and needs special care and attention. You cannot just treat him or her the same way you treat other children. It will require more effort, time, and patience. Dealing with your child may not come quickly. There will be many problems and challenges you might experience. However, do not worry because these will all lead to your child's treatment and recovery.

The following are some of the problems you may face:

- **Lack of communication:** If your child refuses to talk to you, do not worry. As long as you are having quality time and connecting with your child, do not pity yourself for having meaningful conversations. With proper therapy, your kid will be able to open up and talk properly.

- **Fear:** When your child is afraid of something, do not panic. He/she needs attention, so give him/her what he/she needs. Comfort your child and try to explore both the problem and the reason in detail.

- **Taking control:** For easier control and management, do not give your child a choice. Have a prepared list of things you need to ask your child after he/she talks to you. Do not make it too simplistic because it will only frustrate and confuse him/her.

- **Mood swings:** Your child may seemingly be having a good day and suddenly go wrong. You may notice his/her mood stinginess. Do not get upset because they always pass. Instead, check with the others in your family to see if they have experienced similar problems. If you need more details about their experienced, do not hesitate to ask.

- **Losing control:** As the primary parent, when you witness your child losing control, do not get worried. Tell him/her calmly and consistently why you need your room to be kept clean. Show your child that you not afraid to discipline him/her. Ignore his/her tantrums and do the job you are assigned.

- **Deviant behavior:** Your child may not talk to you and behave destructively. Nothing wrong with that since it indicates he/she is listening to you. Sometimes, toddlers have a limited vocabulary and say bad words without meaning to. Talk to your child about it, telling him/her how you feel about him and the bad things he/she is saying. Make it a teaching experience and stop him/her from doing it again.

After following these steps, you will learn to get used to these practices, and dealing with your child's issues will just become routine and hassle-free. It may take a lot of trials and attempts, but they will surely be worth it.

Anticipate Your Child's Behaviour

The first step in dealing with a minor with ADHD is to be aware of the atypical behavior they may manifest. By doing this, you might prevent yourself from reacting impulsively. Thus, your child will be able to receive the best care and support that he or she should get, which is needed for his or her development. Below are the most common behaviors that you can expect to see from your child:

- They often ignore parental instructions.
- They will demand your attention even at inappropriate times. Do not react impulsively, as this may frustrate them and may cause them to act aggressively.
- You will find it challenging to get them to go to bed in the evening.
- They may verbally and physically hurt you when triggers occur.
- They may say and do things impulsively and tactlessly.
- They will be noisy and impatient most of the time.

Be an Optimistic Parent

Yes, your child will have friends, caregivers, and siblings, but no one can give them enough love and support other than you. So when everybody else gives up on their behavior and attitude, you should be positive enough to think that you and your family can get through these challenging times. If people surrounding your child are losing their hopes that they will get better, you should not give up. Here are some specific steps you may undertake to maintain a positive attitude towards your child:

- Believe that your child can get through this. Reassure him or her that no matter what he or she goes through, you will be right behind them to support him or her.

- Appreciate the little things. Yes, your child will become stubborn most of the time, but their simple acts of appreciation for your love and attention should be enough to make your day. Use these times as motivation for you to become more patient and supportive.
- Enjoy what you are doing. So do not get disheartened or upset when things do not turn out the way they are planned. It will get better.

Establish Structures and Patterns

Since children with ADHD are generally disoriented, it will require extraordinary effort to train them to become disciplined and obedient. However, you can introduce them to a structured environment to know what to expect and what is expected. While this may require a lot of effort, it is genuinely effective in helping your child. Below are some ways to do this.

- **Follow a routine.** That may be challenging at first, but you and your child will get used to it after several attempts. Next, schedule your child's ritual for meals, bed, play, and homework. That will help him/her become disciplined.
- **Use timers and clocks as reminders.** Unfortunately, you may not always be around to remind your child, so requiring him or her to use timers and clocks will truly boost his or her development.
- **Do not put so many things on your child's schedule.** Keep it simple and easy to understand. If you make it too complex, your child might not follow it at all.

- **Allot a special place in your home for his or her physical needs.** For example, your child will play a lot and run around, so they must have a permanent space in your house where they can feel free and secure.

Accept the Imperfections of Your Child

Do not expect more from your child. He or she has unique needs. You must treat him or her properly. If you quickly get angry with children because of simple mistakes, it is time that you work on your patience. Your child needs more love and support. To ensure that you understand your child's imperfections, here are some steps to follow:

- **Always give your child another chance.** Whenever your child attempts to do something, yet fails at it, do not give up. Instead, encourage him or her to try again. If you easily give up on your child, they will also give up easily on themselves.
- **Do not reprimand your child for his or her mistakes.** Since your child is unique, many things might be tough for him or her to understand. Do not get upset or angry, as this will only hinder your child's motivation.
- **Be confident in his or her abilities.** Always remind your kid that he or she is capable. Use your child's great attitude and behavior as strengths rather than weaknesses. Through this, your child will become more motivated to overcome his or her condition.

Define the Rules, but Be Flexible When Necessary

As mentioned earlier, children with ADHD find it difficult to follow and obey rules. To make it easier for both you and your child, make sure that the rules are appropriately set and defined. Discipline your child, especially when he or she does not obey you, but ensure that this is done constructively. However, there may be instances wherein your child will demand flexibility. There are going to be situations where you cannot be too firm about sticking with the rules.

- **Easy Rules.** Do not rush your child into following complicated instructions, as this will not help his or her growth.
- **Know when to adjust.** When you are familiar with your child's attitude and behavior, you can easily weigh whether your rules need some adjustment to better cater to your child's needs.
- **Be consistent in teaching your child to obey rules.** Once he or she gets used to your routines, it will not be that demanding for him or her to follow. As a result, you will also not have a difficult time with discipline.

Keeps Distractions Away

Since disciplining children and teaching them to obey rules can be challenging, their environment must be conducive to this learning. Do this by keeping distractions away. These include unnecessary toys, unhealthy food, and harmful objects. Note that children with ADHD usually get attracted to all sorts of things. That is why you must keep your child's environment safe and conducive for growth.

- Surround your child only with things and objects necessary for his or her development. Favorite books and toys will be helpful.
- Keep knives and other hazardous objects out of reach.

Be Patient

Perhaps the most crucial reminder and the most important value you must learn when you have a child with ADHD. If you are generally hot-tempered and impulsive, you have to change your attitude unless you want your child to be the one suffering.

Since you are the one who is more capable of thinking and behaving correctly, take the initiative to be the one to adjust and understand. While your child may annoy you many times during the day, keep your patience long and your head cool. You have to adapt and accommodate, sometimes to a great extent. If you get angry at your child, the anger should be at you for not properly managing and controlling your child. But that is not a reason to strike out at your child.

Chapter 15:
Dealing with Teen with ADHD

I f you work with your child when he is young, and encourage and teach good behavior, chances are you will have a well-behaved teen, but parents who think that because their children have reached their teen years, they no longer have to be vigilant are mistaken. Even before your child is technically a teen as he comes 10 to 12 years old, how he appears to his parents starts to become less critical and is replaced by a need to appeal to his peer group.

This can lead to a whole new set of behavior issues that might take you by surprise, and you may have difficulty dealing with these recent conflicts if you aren't prepared for them. At this stage in a child's life, the thing that matters most is fitting in with the other kids in how you look, sound, and behave. Having ADHD and taking medication during the day or having counseling sessions or lessons with an exceptional tutor do not fit the mold, and your tween will resist all efforts to stick to those routines.

If they do not take the medication, their symptoms will increase, and they will have more problems scholastically, leading to more frustration for them and you. This is a time for compromise, and between you and your child, you will have to find innovative ways to keep the symptoms at bay while still fitting in the crowd at school. Find ways to have them take their medication so no one knows outside of the family. One way of doing this is to take time-release medicines to feel the benefits all day long, and the kids at school don't need to see you taking it. Work with rather than against your tween if you want to get results instead of spending all your time-fighting. This is also a time to pay close attention to the new friends that your child might be making, as attempts to fit in can lead to hanging with the wrong crowd.

As ADHD children approach their teen years, parents will often see a reduction in the child's hyperactivity so that while they might still find it challenging to sit still at school for extended periods, they are more likely to fidget in their seats than they are to get up and walk around and disturb the class. While teens might find it a little easier to control the behaviors associated with having ADHD than younger children, the teen years hold other challenges that might not have been faced when they were more youthful.

With its rush of hormonal changes, adolescence does strange things to most children, and children with ADHD are no different. They struggle with the same issues of needing to fit in and grapple with the same identity crises as other teenagers. However, they may react more intensely to problems than other teens, and their reactions may be more extreme. They are likely to be more embarrassed by their disorder and ask to stop taking their medication because they don't want children at school to see them taking it. This is when it might be a good idea to take the slow-release form of the medication to last all day.

Many teens who have ADHD feel they no longer need to take medication because they can control their symptoms, but this is often not the case. Hence, as parents, you have the task of explaining to an impulsive, inattentive teen why he should continue taking his medication. Try to find a compromise in terms of when it should be taken. A lot of your interaction with your teenager will involve middle of some sort as you attempt to do what's best for them while at the same time avoiding confrontations. Stay calm. Sit and have a conversation with him and try to reach an agreement regarding his medication. Sometimes you might have to agree to let him take a short break from taking them. If his doctor agrees, make a deal with him to stop taking his medication for a month or so in return for a particular behavior.

Make the agreement very specific so he knows precisely what is expected of him in the bargain and what the consequences will be if he does not hold up his end. Sometimes the teenager isn't deliberately avoiding taking his medication; he just forgets to take it because he is preoccupied with other things. Help him remember by sending him text messages or leaving notes for him in places where he can see them.

When your child reaches his teens, it becomes more critical to establish the difference between behavior resulting from having ADHD and behavior that is deliberately disruptive.

Your child will probably continue to struggle at school not because he is not intelligent but because he is disorganized and forgets things quickly. He will still fidget excessively and have trouble paying attention in class. He will fail to complete assignments, and this failure to stick at things will also affect his extra-curricular activities, so he might have trouble keeping his place on sporting teams. Continue to work with him at managing his time productively. Because of the nature of high school, it is harder to manage the time of a teenager, especially after school but don't give up on the schedule just yet.

If your teen does manage to conquer high school and goes on to university, make sure that you prepare thoroughly for that experience. Many teens with ADHD find the transition from high school, where they are closely monitored and have a lot of support, to university, where many independent studies complex. In addition, they have trouble organizing themselves in terms of time management and things like meeting deadlines for handing in papers, setting limits on their extra-curricular activities, and allocating study time because there are so many distractions.

Parents can help them get organized at the beginning of each term or semester. You can also look into private tutoring and help them make special arrangements for the taking of examinations where they may be given a more extended period to complete the exam or be put in a quieter room.

Even teens with ADHD should have more of a say in their own lives and the house rules than they did when they were younger. They can be given a chance to contribute to the list of regulations and the tasks schedule. The parents should, however, still have the final say. Because they are older, it will be harder to "lay down the law" regarding house rules and discipline. They might also be immune to the reward techniques that you used when they were younger, so you will be forced to develop new medication techniques or find ways to make them seem new.

There will be a lot of defiance. Rebellion among teenagers with ADHD is quite common and can also be highly intense. Try to give teens choices but don't leave them open-ended. For instance, when it comes to helping out around the home, let them choose which activity they want to be responsible for. Is it going to be doing the dishes or making the beds? This way, they feel they have input, so there is less chance of defiance and refusal to comply.

Teens with ADHD have a greater tendency to have anger management problems than other teens, so you might want to consider counseling. It is even more futile to lose your temper and engage in a shouting match with your teen than when he was younger, so try as far as possible to avoid that. Remind the teen that they had their chance to contribute to the rules and that what has been agreed to must be followed. Have discussions instead, but still let them know that actions that contradict the house rules will lose phone and computer privileges. Continue an updated version of the method of rewards and consequences that you used when he was younger.

Driving is one of the areas that are fraught with danger for your teen with ADHD. Because they tend to be impulsive and take unnecessary risks, teens with ADHD do not always make the best drivers. They usually have more vehicular accidents than teens without the disorder. Teens with ADHD also get more speeding tickets. They also have trouble staying focused on what they are doing, which is essential when driving, so parents must take the time to instill in their teens the need to be careful on the roads. Ensuring that he sticks to his medication regime helps to cut down on impulsiveness and risk-taking, so it also helps avoid car accidents.

Some stimulants have been found to have weight loss properties, so many teenage girls would be willing to pay handsomely for these pills. Students also use them to keep them awake at night so they can study longer. Your child might be tempted to sell his medication or even give it away to his friends on impulse, so parents must remember to monitor dosage and quantities closely.

Chapter 16:
Treating Your Child Self-Care

I t is better if your child learns to carry out self-care while gaining autonomy, rather than being dependent on your verbal instruction. For example, teach her to wake up to an alarm clock instead of your voice. Always remember to consider your daughter as successful: believe she will learn to put toothpaste on her toothbrush, pour her glass of milk, use a watch, choose her shoes, and dress alone. Even very young children can perform these things, and with your child, you can assume the same.

Your child may not have an age-appropriate accountability background. According to a study, children living with ADHD in their self-management skills are 30 percent behind other children. So unless you tell your child to wash after using the bathroom, pick up after herself, brush her teeth, unzip her jacket, etc., she may not do these things as well as little self-care. Why doesn't she know these basic rituals and habits?

Emphasizing the Advantages

If you try to teach your child self-care, she may respond negatively to your efforts. She may feel like you're pulling away, pushing her to do more work, and taking away your time and companionship. When that happens, she may be balking at the vital thing to do: self-care.

As with weaning, parental efforts to encourage self-care often push away their children. Children are reluctant to give up the support provided by family, so children risk rejection because their parents are not interested in every detail of their lives. In addition, they may be worried that any self-sustaining behavior, particularly of their siblings, will encourage the parents to concentrate on other issues.

Help your child understand the advantages of self-reliance. For example, without you, she can go more places, others won't harp on her so often, and she can perform tasks when there's no help available. You want her to know that she will benefit more than she loses when she displays good self-care. The words you use and your voice tone will affect whether she responds positively, and it's always helpful to note her self-care growth and willingness to help others.

Helping Your Child Follow Through Independently

Helping your daughter do what she says she's going to do without reminding her is vital. Scientists have built a way to help people with their plans to follow through. In this particular way, if you help your child "planning for success," there is an increased chance that she will carry out her plan immediately on her own.

Poor Hygiene

You may keep reminding your child to brush or shower, but this may not be the best solution. Also, if your child depends on your efforts, she's not going to learn how to handle it independently. Also, she will resent the constant reminder and believe you doubt her ability.

Your child knows you're agonizing about her grooming, so failing to meet your expectations could turn into a powerful weapon to threaten you when she's upset. In addition, if she likes the fact that you're worried, she might also be reluctant to give up. Kids are often told that when they overreact to grooming problems, their parents care for them.

Here are some examples:

- Robert was affected by poor modeling; his parents preserved their grooming by copying the mediocre style.
- Delicate motor problems clashed with Michael's self-care; he suffered more than others did, and his parents got accustomed to taking control of themselves.
- Philip felt safer when his body smell kept others at the length of his arm.

Identifying what is hampering the child is essential. Fortunately, children do not always see hygiene in a negative light. For starters, when they get in, kids are often hesitant to get out of the shower. The inability to begin a hygiene-related project seems to have very little to do with the negative.

Solutions

Negative words and coercion can often have a detrimental effect on the hygiene response of your child, and this is often a resistance factor. Checking to see if she washed her hands with soap, or asking her to use it, will only render hand washing an unpleasant activity she would hate. If you experience a power struggle to wash your hands, then you might ask, "What's going on? Are you all right when you let germs live on your paws, or are you upset when you like I'm running you around?" Being positive, maintaining the current pleasure, and complimenting your child's expertise will encourage her to be clean.

Now let's concentrate on brushing teeth. When she wants to take care of her teeth and doesn't know how, you should ask your daughter, "After every meal, the dentist says to clean your teeth. This keeps the teeth healthy and strong." Avoid perpetuating dependency on your child. Instead of brushing the teeth of your child on your own, teach her how to do it, saying, "I can show you how the dentist taught me." Help her recognize that when she manages her own task, she is taking good care of herself. Healthy teeth need less repair (which is never pleasant), and when others see her good smile and note how great she looks, your child will surely like it.

However, sometimes your child may be testing to see if she has the right to say no to a request for hygiene, and you may recognize the problem rather than insist on it. When her health is bad for a short time, the world won't end. As the saying goes, "Choose your battles." Your child's poor hygiene has little to do with failing to understand the effects of their actions.

Ostracizing

You may find it necessary to ostracize your daughter to overcome her lack of hygiene in extreme circumstances. Because it's required to be considerate of others, you might suggest, "We'd love to have you join us, but only if you're able to shower and get ready in clean clothes." If she keeps refusing, you might ask, "Is there any reason to create this kind of family problem? Were you distracted by something else?"

If there is no improvement, and if someone can stay with her when you go out, you might leave your child behind. Of course you will think about the family budget if you have to hire someone to monitor her. You may allow her to pay the sitter with her money (or sell some of her toys if she doesn't have cash). Yes, she has the power to sabotage, but she misses the excursion and helps with her funds to offset the inconvenience. She then decides whether hygiene should be disregarded or obeyed.

Difficulties with dress

Your child is likely to have packing, buttoning, and zipping issues, so she must learn those skills. She might not be enthusiastic about giving up your help, unfortunately. For example, she might yell out, "Ma!" and then lift her leg calmly and wait until you put on her sock. Of course, you feel negligent if you don't support her, but you don't perpetuate laziness or superiority by providing such assistance.

Alternatively, just offer enough help to keep advancing slowly. Unless you assist as soon as your daughter cries or says, "I can't," her self-care abilities will fail. Asking her to explain why she cannot is a constructive first move that will keep the ball in her hands.

Solutions

It takes time to help your child develop self-help skills. If you're hurried and pressured to get things done, you're not going to enjoy the luxury of waiting for her to solve problems. She may doubt that she can learn to meet expectations quickly enough and may become disrupted and discouraged. When you prepare, this dilemma can be eliminated, and things will work better. For starters, the night before, when there's time to work together, you should discuss clothing options. It beats becoming frenzied when time is short in the morning.

If your child has more authority over her clothes, she may show more interest and cooperation. For example, you might just point out, "It's cold outside," instead of telling her what to wear on a cold day. This will help her feel that she has control over her outfit selection. In addition, she can learn to check the weather herself as she gets older.

Chapter 17:
Adjusting Your Child to School

T he behavior of your child at home and his actions at school are significantly different. Why are there issues with one atmosphere and not the other? For example, if your son has behavioral or learning difficulties, transitioning to school may be challenging. He may display a much more extreme ADHD attitude when at school than at home. On the other hand, if he is knowledgeable or satisfied by the classroom arrangement, the school may be far less troublesome.

Who Does the Accommodating?

Some ADHD therapies recommend programs to respond to the child's ADHD requirements. The assumptions about ADHD influence the direction parents take with their child's issues in school. They want the school to provide permanent accommodation when they believe that ADHD is a permanent biological disability. We expect that they will always rely on special services for their child. We agree that their child will always need a private assistant in the classroom, a second set of books, extra time to finish the job, desired seating, and close monitoring by all concerned.

Your child can learn to stop showing ADHD symptoms, and from the extra help he's used to, you can wean him. Although your son may potentially benefit from special services, you may concentrate on finding existing deficiencies that hold him back from school opportunities. Then you can work diligently to reduce the need for a personalized program.

When you believe your son is unable to make progress without support, try to limit how long he will need it and try to reduce step-by-step. For example, if he was initially able to benefit from a classroom helper, ask yourself, what must he learn so he no longer needs such accommodation?

Learning in Groups

He has to make a considerable change from the life he is used to when your child begins school. He has to detach himself from you and meet the demands of outsiders who want full compliance. He has to leave the safety of one-to-one contact and his comfortable home environment to spend most of his time mixing in with many others fighting for scarce attention.

You can spot the children with ADHD in any school classroom. Just wait for the teacher to give the "whole class" instruction to get something done. Then look at who's fidgeting, squirming, and not engaging. While the other kids follow the teacher's instructions and listen to her speak, a child with ADHD is often unruly and having fun with others. The whole class is interrupted by his antics. His team approach to everything a significant drawback to his school success. The teacher is going to think about how he will affect the of others.

The Difficulty of Groups

For any of the following reasons, classes may be challenging for your child.

- He feels disconnected from the class and his peers.
- He objects to the bullying that takes place.
- The class is afraid he wants to expose their shortcomings.

- At home, the behavior of your child often run counter to the family group. She may be off doing her own thing when the family is together, waiting for her to join. He often intrudes when not invited. He wants to transfer attention to him when others have the limelight. Parents will get used to this attitude and brush it off, but an instructor will not. Your child must learn to fit into group settings.

Solutions

It's great to spend time with your child alone to create trust. However, it's also essential to give him plenty of opportunities to be part of a group. Bring the family together to help him practice the skills in a classroom group he will need. Suppose family members engage in activities that separate them from each other, such as watching TV in different rooms. In that case, the child will struggle to know how to communicate and get along in groups. Practice is the only way the child can learn how to communicate successfully with others. Aim to have "small group" meetings to share thoughts and feelings. Ask him about his day and the things that are important to him.

Enable him to observe and engage in a dialogue held between at least three people to develop team manners. Your child may quickly drop out of such a discussion if he is not especially interested in the topic. Yet you can gradually encourage him to pay more attention and take turns in the conversation. The key is to make team interaction a joy and keep him active. You will do this easily by promoting appropriate behavior: reassure him that others enjoy his company and are delighted to be a member of the group as he (a) builds on the topic in a clear and meaningful way rather than going off track and (b) waits patiently until others finish before speaking.

Other reasons for school difficulty

In addition to difficulties functioning in teams, children living with ADHD often have trouble in other ways. If something hinders your child's success in school, find as many contributing factors as each requires a different solution.

Learning Difficulty

About one-third of children living with ADHD have a learning disability. If your son has a specific learning difficulty, such as dyslexia (i.e., deficiency of adolescent reading), make sure to enroll him in a comprehensive curriculum. Work closely with the school and probably a professional mentor to ensure he has the support he needs. It is not shocking that children with learning difficulties are more likely to show symptoms ADHD, and their likelihood of success is lower. They are shielded from revealing their inadequacies by their indifference and disobedience. ADHD activity, though, typically aggravates the issue. No one learns well without experience, and training slows as the focus shifts to the infant's actions.

Fear of Failure

A child's worry about his lack of skill can cause schoolwork ADHD behavior. For example, you might find that your child neglects to write down his homework or bring home needed supplies. Still, these oversights have the powerful effect of protecting him (at least temporarily) from struggles and disappointments. Breaking the rules doesn't help him excel, so why follow the rules or play at all? Living in such oblivion saves him from feeling like a loser.

For your child, schoolwork can sometimes be so threatening and uncomfortable that he grasps his pencil so tightly that he hurts his hand. He will second-guess his responses and lose his thought process and ask you for the solution so he will not make a mistake. He can overreact, slap you or himself, and say he's dumb. But such anger only hurts the results, even though it often allows others to ease their expectations. It can free him from the stress he faces by speeding through a task or giving up. On the other hand, failure can also benefit him by delaying critical judgment for the lousy execution of the task.

Because he doesn't want to reveal his weakness, the kid may not ask questions in class. Similarly, if you check in with him and offer to help when he's doing homework, he might say impatiently, "I know, I know," so you'll leave him alone. The fact is that because it makes him feel insecure, and that means incompetent.

Solutions

If your son is upset by the possibility of defeat, it is imperative to respond appropriately to his mistakes so he will be more accepting of his faults. Nonetheless, being overly excited over small successes may not motivate him to work hard either. Instead, let him realize that people have to compete to achieve in meaningful ways most of the time while going through many hurdles.

The Benefits of Dependency

Your child's dependency on you has security and power. He will prevent venturing into the unknown by behaving in ways that trigger your protective instincts and have you take care of problems for him. Relationships are all about getting relief from difficulties for many kids with ADHD. However, this leaves valuable little time to enjoy the company in more mature ways.

As school can be your child's first experience away from you, it can cause issues for both of you with separation, alienation, and dependence. While he may expect the same care at school that you give him at home, that same amount of attention is impossible in a classroom of twenty-five students. He can feel even more depressed at school because he worries that he doesn't get enough adult time at home. He may want to go to school, or you may have go to get him.

The school issues of your ADHD child may be a way to make sure you don't worry about him. Problems are like a magnet; they will pull you in. Have you ever had to leave work because you received your child's call from school? He doesn't seem to know the consequences of his actions, so you come to his aid, pick up the pieces, give him a pep talk, and maybe protect him. It's hard for him to give up these privileges, and they can overwhelm the whole family.

Nonetheless, it is common for parents to be worried that others will blame them for not doing enough, so they are doing even more. To prevent adverse school effects from happening, teachers go to great lengths. After hearing his grievances and threats to give up, they end up doing much of the homework. While they are fearful of unfinished work and procrastination, their attempts at completing the work do very little to improve academic ability or independence.

Social Problems

When in the starting lineup, everybody wants to be part of a team. But what about the benched players? If your child fails academically or socially and doesn't join in, he becomes like the player at the far end of the bench. The excitement and interest in what is happening, like the player who never gets into the game, is likely to disappear. He can feel uncomfortable and even relatively isolated if he doesn't get along with teachers or peers in any setting. This may boost his desire to escape and disturb, and he may have trouble going through the day of class. During adolescence, when social relations become even more important, these kinds of problems can intensify.

Chapter 18:
ADHD Child Routine

For children with ADHD, daily preparation requires a healthy balance between structure and fun. Try those tips for a good and smooth day for you and your kids. There's no ideal plan for raising an ADHD child, but following a comprehensive, organized schedule, your child will be able to complete his or her chores and still have some fun.

These approaches will direct you when creating an ADHD plan for your family:

- Build good habits. When a behavior is a habit, achievement takes far less focus. However, when you understand the overall routine for your boy, stress just one behavior at a time, such as putting his toys away before bedtime. Choose the one with the most significant influence, Dr. Arnold suggests, and first focus on the one.

- Set achievable goals. Break more giant blocks of time into smaller, doable tasks in your ADHD program. For example, rather than setting aside an hour for general chores, select a straightforward, manageable task, such as feeding the family dog, followed by something more fun — or just a break.

- Schedule fitness opportunities. Physical exercise is helpful for children with ADHD, so always aim to make room for outdoor activity in your schedule, if possible. For bad weather days, schedule indoor options, such as fitness-oriented games like Wii Fit tennis.

- Write down your daily plan. For children with ADHD, written instructions or checklists with specific steps are much more effective than verbal instructions as they are easier to recall and study. Written directions also, Arnold says, have less emotional stimuli for both parent and child. Giving short, age-appropriate lists of activities to be completed to children with ADHD — or small steps towards an enormous task — can keep them on track. Young kids may need photos to help them achieve the tasks on their list.

- Create a daily reward system. Children with ADHD also react well to a simple incentive, such as stars for completed tasks and a regular star-quota for a favorite activity. Older children also enjoy a chance to save their principals for a bigger reward at the end of the week.

- Include your child. It is a good idea to give your child some restricted, age-appropriate choices in the schedule.

"With obligation comes the luxury of having your timetable," Dr, Arnold points out. So, for instance, if your child prefers showering in the morning but cannot do so and meet specific deadlines, move the showering to another place on the list.

Creating a daily ADHD plan

In light of the above guidelines, you can build a more tailored schedule for your child's needs. Not all of the tasks mentioned below should be included per day. For example, if you need to do a few morning errands, you may want to miss home chores and incorporate outdoor play into your schedule for errand-running.

Morning Routine

- Wake up. Sticking to the same time every makes mornings easier. Older children may use an alarm. Younger children can be softly awakened up with your touch and sing or call their name.
- Morning hygiene. Older kids will need to add "take medication" to the list.
- Breakfast. Give favored balanced food options but stay clear of those with coloring artificial foods. Dr. Arnold says children with ADHD benefit from additive-free diets.
- Pet care. If your child has a cat, it's a good time to give him food or water and clean his cage.
- Morning study or chores. If your child is not going to school that day, it's an excellent time to get some tasks done. Choose a particular, straightforward job or do some homework, then break for play or relaxation. You may want to make a weekly chore chart to write down a particular task for each day.

After-school Routine

- Snack. Children with ADHD often do better with snacks or small, balanced, regular meals.
- Outside play or sports. While children with ADHD benefit from the structure, it is also necessary to have some free play like romping on a playground.
- Nap. This is as needed and age-appropriate.

- Homework or chores. Keep in mind that children coming home from school may need to take a break and have a snack before returning to school, but you must decide based on your child's needs and when any ADHD medication will wear off. Homework or tutoring is better performed when the meds are still working.

- Play or relaxation. Given that excessive television is not a good idea, Dr. Arnold says that if children enjoy watching such television shows, it can be a pleasant diversion and incentive to complete work or work.

- Clean up. Provide clear instructions for a particular mission again. Instead of saying, "Pick up your things," try, "Let's place all the toys back on the shelf."

Dinner Routine

- Hire them to help prepare dinner. Involve kids with age-appropriate steps. You should build a checklist relating to dinner with actions such as "set the table" or "make a family salad" to help them along.

- Schedule a relaxing after dinner. "Children with ADHD have difficulty calming down," Dr. Arnold says. They still need your support, even though they are tired. If you're used to watching TV at night, pick calmer shows; light comedies are all right but avoid drama, he says. Another good choice is a quiet board game.

Evite behaviors such as competitive sports or video games that energize.

Bedtime Routine

- Get ready for bed. This is another good time for a guided checklist, like "shower or bathe, wash the hair, brush the teeth, put on PJs, and put dirty clothes in the hamper."
- Put out clothes for tomorrow. Choosing an outfit and putting it where your child will find it quickly allows for a smoother morning routine. Also, the evening is an excellent time to collect homework and put it all in the school bag the next day.
- Include calming, wind-down events. For example, try a list to relax music together, or give a mini-massage to your kid. "Fifteen minutes of massage is of interest to children with ADHD," Dr. Arnold says.
- Use firm pressure for better results. For example, Dr. Arnold suggests rolling up and down a tennis ball behind the child. Often helpful for kids with ADHD are calming music and recorded relaxation programs.
- Set a sleep schedule. Children with ADHD frequently have trouble sleeping, but still they must be on a daily sleep schedule. Check that you have a fixed time for bed and wake up.

If your child has problems with sleep, Arnold suggests talking to your child's doctor as medication may help. Kids with ADHD can be great fun with their high energy and imagination as they fly through their day. Your role is simply to have a versatile framework, healthy snacks, and much love.

Conclusion

T hank you very much for making it to the end portion of the Parenting a Child with ADHD. Let's hope it was full of information and delivered all needed the tools you require to attain your goals, regardless of what they may be.

All the suggestions and solutions provided in this book focus only on one thing: to provide your child with the necessary help. It is all about how your child can opt for adequate self-control and self-care in all types of situations, despite their symptoms of ADHD. It is essential for dealing with your child's present and having a healthy and bright future. Keep following all the recommended suggestions correctly. You will be able to develop an extraordinary bond with your ADHD child, a kind of relationship where both of you will respect each other. Try not to take excessive stress.

Children suffering from the symptoms of ADHD already experience a great deal of stress in their daily lives as they try their best to cope with everything that keeps happening around them. However, if you just abide by the strategies provided in this book, you will get the opportunity to make all their daily struggle a lot easier. Children are bound to struggle with being organized, finishing the simplest tasks, or even remembering stuff. But never give up hope.

You have to keep full faith in your child. The related symptoms of ADHD are different for every child. Some children might wake up in a bad mood in the morning, while others might have mood swings during the evening. You will have to monitor all your child's symptoms correctly and think about how you can make the most challenging things a bit easier.

Children suffering from the symptoms of ADHD often feel cluttered. It creates a great deal of confusion, which might make them overwhelmed. So, you will have to stress being organized. It is essential if you want your child to get done with their studies and adequately finish all their tasks on a timely basis. Some ideas:

- Try to use pocket folders in various colors. For instance, in the red-colored folder, you can arrange all the homework assignments for your child. You can make another folder for organizing all the graded papers returned by the teachers. If your child has to deal with a significant number of subjects, you can create various folders for different topics to make things easier.
- You can also use color-coding to separate all those tasks your child has to complete.

It is your duty to keep your child's study desk organized so your ADHD child wants to study. Make your child understand the importance of being organized and make them clear all the clutter on their study table. You can also keep a basket beside the study desk so that he/she can throw away all the things they do not need. You will have to make sure the place where your child studies has a fresh vibe. Also, the location needs to be comfortable. As your child organizes his/her room, you can spend some time with them and make the whole thing a fun activity.

Parents of ADHD children seem to be very over-protective. While doing so, you might start thinking of other people as your enemy. However, in actuality, this is not the case. You might get the feeling that the members of your family or people surrounding your ADHD child are not providing him/her with enough care. But you need to understand that every individual comes with their way of caring. However, if you strongly feel that an individual is not providing enough care, you can indulge in a proper form of communication. There is no need to treat that person as your enemy. You simply converse with them regarding your child, his strengths and weaknesses, along with his preferences.

When you are with your ADHD child, who seems to be very hyperactive most of the time and keeps showcasing impulsive behavior, it might result in a power struggle. Just do not answer every tantrum your ADHD child throws. You will have to learn how to let go of small things to alleviate your level of stress successfully. Also, children who have ADHD do not do well with direct commands. So, do not command your child to do something; instead, try to explain what needs to be done.

It is essential to dwelling on positivity as you handle your ADHD child. You will have to provide feedback. Indeed, it might seem impossible at times to focus on positivity. So, as a parent, you will have to develop an outlet where you can easily express all your concerns and worries. Opt for online groups if you need more help.

CPSIA information can be obtained
at www.ICGtesting.com
Printed in the USA
LVHW081918190621
690650LV00006B/524